MW01269128

macOS Sonoma User Guide

Your Essential Guide to macOS Sonoma

Steve Rufus

Contents

Get to know the desktop

What's in the menu bar?

The menu bar runs along the top of the screen on your Mac. Use the menus and icons in the menu bar to choose commands, perform tasks, and check status.

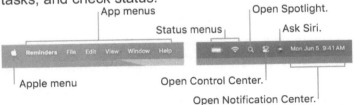

App menus

Status menus

Open Spotlight.

Ask Siri.

Apple menu

Open Control Center.

Open Notification Center.

You can set an option to automatically hide the menu bar so it's shown only when you move the pointer to the top of the screen.

Apple menu

The Apple menu , located in the top-left corner of the screen, contains commands for things you do frequently, such as update apps, open System Settings, lock your screen, or shut down your Mac.

App menus

App menus are located next to the Apple menu. The name of the app you're using appears in bold, followed by other menus, often with standard names such as File, Edit, Format, or Window. Each app has a Help menu to make it easy to get information about using the app.

Each menu contains commands, many of which are available in most apps. For example, the Open command is often in the File menu.

Status menus

Toward the right end of the menu bar are items (sometimes called status menus), typically represented by icons, that let you check the status of your Mac (such as the battery charge) or customize features (such as keyboard brightness).

7

To show more details or options, click a status menu icon. For example, click Wi-Fi 🛜 to show a list of available networks, or click Display 🖥 to turn Dark Mode or Night Shift on or off. You can choose which items to show in the menu bar.

To rearrange status menus, press and hold the Command key while you drag an icon. To quickly remove a status menu, press and hold the Command key while you drag the icon out of the menu bar.

Spotlight

If the Spotlight icon 🔍 is shown in the menu bar, click the icon to search for items on your Mac and the web.

Control Center

Click the Control Center icon 🎛 to open Control Center, where you can access features you use often, such as AirDrop, AirPlay, Focus, and more.

Siri

If the Siri icon ⚫ is shown in the menu bar, click the icon to use Siri to do things like open files or apps, or to find things on your Mac or on the internet.

Notification Center

At the right end of the menu bar, click the date and time to open Notification Center, where you can view appointments, notes, weather, and more, and catch up on notifications you missed.

Work on the desktop

At the top of the screen is the menu bar and at the bottom is the Dock. In between is what's called the *desktop*. The desktop is where you do your work.

Change the desktop picture

You can choose a different macOS desktop picture—dynamic ones automatically change throughout the day—or use one of your own photos.

Change the desktop appearance

You can choose a light or dark appearance for the menu bar, desktop picture, Dock, and built-in apps.

Use notifications on the desktop

Notifications appear in the top-right corner of the desktop to let you know about upcoming events, incoming emails or messages, and more; you can ask for a reminder, reply to a message, and more, right from the notification. You can customize how and when notifications appear. To pause them when you need to concentrate on a task, turn on a Focus.

Organize files on the desktop

If you like to keep files handy on the desktop, you can use stacks to neatly group files by type or other criteria along one side of the desktop—whenever you add a file to the desktop, it automatically goes into a stack.

Find a window on the desktop

If your desktop is covered by open windows, you can use Mission Control to move them aside to get to the desktop, or to show a simple view of everything that's open on the desktop, so it's easy to spot the window you need.

Use multiple desktops

You can create additional desktop spaces to organize tasks on specific desktops. For example, you can manage email on one desktop while focusing on a project using another desktop, and easily switch between the two. You can even customize each desktop to suit the task you're working on.

Search with Spotlight

Spotlight can help you quickly find apps, documents, emails, and other items on your Mac. With Siri Suggestions, you can also get news, sports scores, weather conditions, stock prices, and more. Spotlight can even perform calculations and conversions for you.

Search for something

1. On your Mac, do one of the following:
   - Click the Spotlight icon Q (if shown) in the menu bar.
   - Press Command-Space bar.
   - Press Q (if available) in the row of function keys on the keyboard.
2. You can drag the Spotlight window anywhere on the desktop.
   Tip: If the Spotlight icon isn't in the menu bar, add it using Control Center settings.
3. In the search field, type what you're looking for—results appear as you type.
   Spotlight lists top matches first; click a top match to preview or open it. Spotlight also suggests variations of your search;

those results appear in Spotlight or on the web.

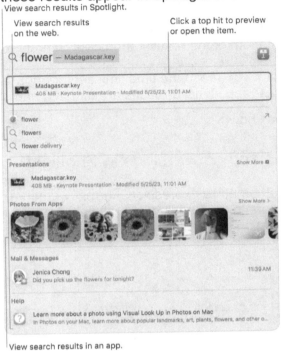

View search results in Spotlight.

View search results
on the web.

Click a top hit to preview
or open the item.

View search results in an app.

4. In the results, do any of the following:

○ *See results of a suggested search in Spotlight:* Click an item preceded by the Spotlight icon.

○ *See results of a suggested search on the web:* Click an item followed by an arrow icon.

○ *Open an item:* Double-click it. Or select the item, then press the Return key.
This action may open an app, such as Messages, Help Viewer, and more.

○ *Turn a setting on or off:* Click to turn a setting (such as VoiceOver) on or off when you search for it in Spotlight.

○ *Take a quick action:* When you type a phone number, email, date, or time, you may be able to take a quick action—such as making a FaceTime call or sending an email.

○ *Show the location of a file on your Mac:* Select the file, then press and hold the Command key. The file's location appears at the bottom of the preview.

11

- *Copy an item:* Drag a file to the desktop or a Finder window.
- *See all results from your Mac in the Finder:* Scroll to the bottom of the results, then click Search in Finder.

During downtime, or if you reach the time limit set for apps in Screen Time settings, app icons in results are dimmed and an hourglass icon  is shown.

Get calculations and conversions in Spotlight

You can enter a mathematical expression, currency amount, temperature, and more in the Spotlight search field, and get a conversion or calculation right in the same place.

- *Calculations:* Enter a mathematical expression, such as 956*23.94 or 2020/15.
- *Currency conversions:* Enter a currency amount, such as $100, 100 yen, or "300 krone in euros."
- *Temperature conversions:* Enter a temperature, such as 98.8F, 32C, or "340K in F."
- *Measurement conversions:* Enter a measurement, such as 25 lbs, 54 yards, 23 stone, or "32 ft to meters."
- *World clock conversions:* Enter a phrase about a time in a location, such as "time in Paris" or "Japan local time."

You can include or exclude specific folders, disks, or types of information (such as email or messages) from Spotlight searches.

If you want Spotlight to search content only on your Mac and not include results from the web, you can turn off Siri Suggestions for Spotlight.

Quickly change settings

Control Center on Mac gives you quick access to key macOS settings—such as AirDrop, Wi-Fi, or Focus. You can customize Control Center to add other items, such as accessibility shortcuts, battery status, or fast user switching.

An orange dot ● next to the Control Center icon ◉ in the menu bar indicates the microphone on your Mac is in use; an arrow ◁ (macOS 14 or later) indicates your location is in use. When you open Control Center, the top of the window may contain a field that shows which apps are using your microphone, location, or camera. You can click that field to open the Privacy window, which may have additional information (macOS 13.3 or later).

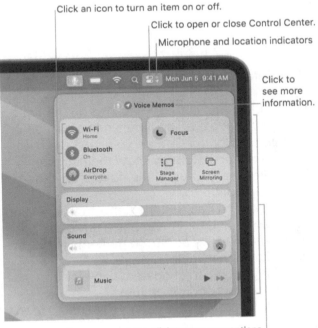

Click an icon to turn an item on or off.

Click to open or close Control Center.

Microphone and location indicators

Click to see more information.

For some controls, click to see more options.
For Stage Manger, click to turn it on or off.

13

Use Control Center

1. On your Mac, click Control Center ⬭ in the menu bar.
2. Do any of the following with items in Control Center:
    - Drag a slider to increase or decrease a setting—for example, drag the Sound slider to adjust the volume on your Mac.
    - Click an icon to turn a feature on or off—for example, click AirDrop or Bluetooth® to turn it on or off.
    - Click an item (or its arrow ❯) to show more options—for example, click Focus to show your Focus list and turn a Focus on or off, or click Screen Mirroring to choose a target display.

Tip: If you often use an item, you can drag it from Control Center to the menu bar, to keep it handy there. To remove the item from the menu bar, press and hold the Command key while you drag the item out of the menu bar.

Customize Control Center

1. On your Mac, choose Apple menu > System Settings, then click Control Center ⬭ in the sidebar. (You may need to scroll down.)
2. Choose settings for the items in these sections on the right.
    - *Control Center Modules:* The items in this section are always shown in Control Center; you can't remove them. You can choose to also show them in the menu bar. Click the pop-up menu next to an item, then choose an option.
    - *Other Modules:* You can add the items in this section to Control Center and the menu bar. Turn each option below an item on or off. Some items may have additional settings available.
    - *Menu Bar Only:* You can choose options for the menu bar clock, and add other items (such as Spotlight, Siri, Time Machine, and VPN status) to the menu bar.

Use Siri

You can use Siri on your Mac to do everyday tasks like setting up a meeting, opening an app, or getting quick answers to questions.

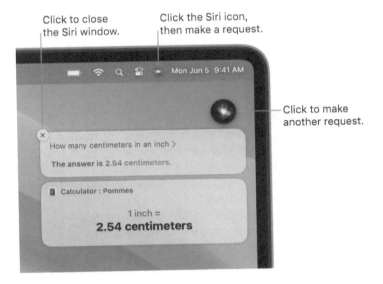

Click to close the Siri window.

Click the Siri icon, then make a request.

Click to make another request.

Turn on Siri

1. On your Mac, choose Apple menu > System Settings, then click Siri & Spotlight in the sidebar. (You may need to scroll down.)
2. On the right, turn on Ask Siri if it's not already on, then click Enable.
   If you try to activate Siri when the option isn't selected, you're prompted to enable Siri. You must be connected to the internet to use Siri.
3. If you're asked if you want to improve Siri and Dictation, do one of the following:
   - *Share audio recordings:* Click Share Audio Recordings to allow Apple to store audio of your Siri and Dictation interactions from your Mac. Apple may review a sample of stored audio.
   - *Don't share audio recordings:* Click Not Now.

4. If you change your mind later and want to share or stop sharing audio recordings, choose Apple menu > System Settings, then click Privacy & Security in the sidebar. (You may need to scroll down.) Click Analytics & Improvements on the right, then turn on or off the Improve Siri & Dictation option.
   Note: You can delete the audio interactions (which are associated with a random identifier and less than six months old) whenever you like.
5. Do any of the following:
   o *Use "Hey Siri" or "Siri":* If available for your device and language, turn on the "Listen for" option or choose the phrase you want to speak to start using Siri. When this option is on and you turn on "Allow Siri when locked," you can also use Siri even if your Mac is locked or in sleep.
   o *Set a keyboard shortcut:* Click the "Keyboard shortcut" pop-up menu, then choose a shortcut to activate Siri or create your own.

      Tip: If is available in the row of function keys, you can press and hold it to activate Siri or use the keyboard shortcut.
   o *Choose how Siri speaks:* Click the Language pop-up menu, then choose a language. Click Select next to "Siri voice" to hear a preview, then choose the voice that you want Siri to use from the Voice Variety options and the Siri Voice options. (Some languages may only have one option.)
   o *Mute Siri:* Click Siri Responses, then turn off "Voice feedback"—the response from Siri is shown in the Siri window but not spoken.
   o *Show what Siri says on screen:* Click Siri Responses, then turn on "Always show Siri captions."
   o *Show what you say on screen:* Click Siri Responses, then turn on "Always show speech."

Tip: To add Siri to the menu bar, choose Apple menu > System Settings, then click Control Center in the sidebar. (You may need to scroll down.) Go to Menu Bar Only on the right, then choose Show in Menu Bar next to Siri.

Activate Siri

Note: You must be connected to the internet to use Siri.

1. To activate Siri on your Mac, do any of the following:
   - Press and hold 🎤 if available in the row of function keys or use the keyboard shortcut as specified in Siri & Spotlight settings.
   - Click Siri ⬤ in the menu bar. If it's not shown, you can add it using Control Center settings.
   - Tap Siri in the Touch Bar (if your Mac has a Touch Bar).
   - Say "Hey Siri" or "Siri" (if this option is available and turned on in Siri & Spotlight settings).
2. Make a request—for example, "Set up a meeting at 9" or "What was the score for last night's game?"

If you have Location Services turned on, the location of your device at the time you make a request will be determined.

Turn off Siri

1. On your Mac, choose Apple menu > System Settings, then click Siri & Spotlight ⬤ in the sidebar. (You may need to scroll down.)
2. On the right, turn off Ask Siri.

Get notifications

In Notification Center on your Mac, you can catch up on notifications you missed and use widgets to view appointments, birthdays, the weather, top headlines, and more right from the desktop.

Click the date and time to
open Notification Center.

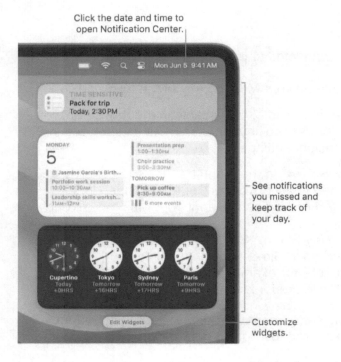

See notifications
you missed and
keep track of
your day.

Customize
widgets.

Open or close Notification Center on your Mac

On your Mac, do any of the following:

- *Open Notification Center:* Click the date and time in the menu bar, or swipe left with two fingers from the right edge of the trackpad.
- *Close Notification Center:* Click anywhere on the desktop, click the date and time in the menu bar, or swipe right with two fingers toward the right edge of the trackpad.

Use notifications in Notification Center on your Mac

In Notification Center, move the pointer over a notification, then do any of the following:

- *Expand or collapse a stack of notifications:* If an app's notifications are grouped, multiple notifications are stacked. To expand the stack and show all of the notifications, click anywhere in the top notification. To collapse the stack, click "Show less."

- *Take action:* Click the action. For example, click Snooze in a notification from the Calendar app, or click Reply in a notification from the Mail app.

  If an action has an arrow ⌄ next to it, click the arrow for more options. For example, to reply to a call using the Messages app, click the arrow next to Decline, then choose Reply with Message.
- *See more details:* Click the notification to open the item in the app. If an arrow ⟩ is shown to the right of the app name, click the arrow to show details in the notification.

- *Change an app's notification settings:* If an arrow ⟩ is shown to the right of the app name, click the arrow, click the More button ···, then choose to mute or turn off notifications, or show the app's notification settings in Notifications settings.
- *Clear a single notification or all notifications in a stack:* Click the Clear or Clear All button ⊗.

Use widgets in Notification Center on your Mac

In Notification Center, do any of the following:

- *See more details:* Click anywhere in a widget to open the related settings, app, or webpage. For example, click in a Clock widget to open Date & Time settings, the Reminders widget to open the Reminders app, or the Weather widget to open the browser and view the complete forecast.
- *Resize a widget:* Control-click a widget, then choose a different size.
- *Remove a widget:* Press and hold the Option key while you move the pointer over the widget, then click the Remove button ⊖.

You can change which widgets are shown in Notification Center and customize them.

Tip: If you need to minimize distractions by silencing all notifications—or allowing only certain notifications to appear—use a Focus, such as Do Not Disturb or Work.

Open apps from the Dock

The Dock on the Mac desktop is a convenient place to access apps and features that you're likely to use every day—for example, Launchpad and the Trash.

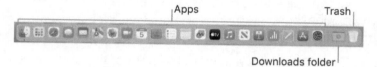

Apps   Trash

Downloads folder

The Dock can show up to three recently used apps that aren't already in it and a folder for items you download from the internet. By default, the Dock is located along the bottom edge of the screen, but you can set an option to show it along the left or right edge instead.

Open items in the Dock

In the Dock on your Mac, do any of the following:

- *Open an app:* Click the app icon. For example, to open the Finder, click the Finder icon in the Dock.
- *Open a file in an app:* Drag the file over an app's icon. For example, to open a document you created in Pages, drag the document over the Pages icon in the Dock.
- *Show an item in the Finder:* Command-click the item's icon.
- *Switch to the previous app and hide the current app:* Option-click the current app's icon.
- *Switch to another app and hide all other apps:* Option-Command-click the icon of the app you want to switch to.

Take other actions for items in the Dock

In the Dock on your Mac, do any of the following:

- *Display a shortcut menu of actions:* Control-click an item to display its shortcut menu, then choose an action, such as Show Recents, or click a filename to open the file.

- *Force an app to quit:* If an app stops responding, Control-click the app's icon, then choose Force Quit (you may lose unsaved changes).

Add, remove, or rearrange Dock items

On your Mac, do any of the following:

- *Add an item to the Dock:* Drag apps to the left side of (or above) the line that separates the recently used apps. Drag files and folders to the right side of (or below) the other line that separates recently used apps. An alias for the item is placed in the Dock.

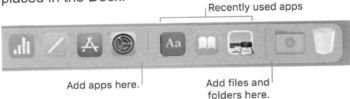

Recently used apps

Add apps here.   Add files and folders here.

When you drag a folder to the Dock, you can view it as a stack. By default, the Dock comes with a Downloads folder.
- *Remove an item from the Dock:* Drag the item out of the Dock until Remove is shown. Only the alias is removed; the actual item remains on your Mac.
  If you accidentally remove an app icon from the Dock, it's easy to put it back (the app is still on your Mac). Open the app to make its icon appear again in the Dock. Control-click the app's icon, then choose Options > Keep in Dock.
- *Rearrange items in the Dock:* Drag an item to a new location.

Tip: If you use Handoff, the Handoff icon of the app you're using on your iPhone, iPad, iPod touch, or Apple Watch appears near the right end of the Dock.

Customize the Dock

1. On your Mac, choose Apple menu > System Settings, then click Desktop & Dock in the sidebar. (You may need to scroll down.)

21

2. Below Dock on the right, change the options you want. For example, you can change how items appear in the Dock, adjust its size, locate it along the left or right edge of the screen, or even hide it.

To learn about the options, click the Help button (?) at the bottom of the window.

Tip: To quickly adjust the Dock's size, move the pointer over the separator line in the Dock until a double arrow appears, then click and drag the pointer down or up. You can Control-click the separator to access other actions from the shortcut menu.

You can use keyboard shortcuts to navigate to the Dock. Press Fn-Control-F3 to move to the Dock. Then use the Left Arrow and Right Arrow keys to move from icon to icon. Press Return to open an item.

A red badge on an icon in the Dock indicates you need to take one or more actions in an app or System Settings. For example, a red badge on the Mail icon in the Dock indicates you have new emails to read.

Organize your files in the Finder

The Finder is the home base for your Mac. The Finder icon looks like a blue smiling face; click the icon in the Dock to open a Finder window.

You use Finder windows to organize and access almost everything on your Mac.

Choose how you want to view items.

Select a file, then share or tag it.

Finder sidebar

See your stuff

Click items in the Finder sidebar to see your files, apps, downloads, and more. To make the sidebar even more useful, customize it. To make the Finder window even more useful, show the Preview pane.

Access everything, everywhere

Use iCloud Drive to store files and folders in iCloud. You can access them on any device where you're signed in with the same Apple ID.

Organize with folders or tags

If you like organizing your files in folders, you can do that. You can create new folders in your Documents folder, on the desktop, or in iCloud Drive.

You can also tag files and folders with helpful keywords to make them easier to find.

Clean a messy desktop

Stacks helps you keep files organized in tidy groups on the desktop. You can group stacks by kind, date, or tags. When you group by kind, all your images go in one stack, presentations in another, and so on. Any new files you add go immediately to the correct stack—helping you keep everything in order automatically.

Choose your view

You can choose how you view the items in Finder windows. For example, you don't have to view your items in a list—Gallery view lets you flip through your files and folders visually.

Send files or folders

You can send a copy of a file or folder to a nearby Mac, iPhone, or iPad right from the Finder. Click AirDrop in the sidebar to get started.

You can also select a file or folder in the Finder, then click the Share button ⬆️ (or use the Touch Bar) to send it using Mail, AirDrop, Messages, and more. If you don't see the Share button, click the More Toolbar Items button ≫ at the end of the toolbar.

Share files or folders

You can work on a file or folder in iCloud Drive with other people who use iCloud. Select a file or folder in the Finder, click the Share button ⬆️ (or use the Touch Bar), then choose Share File or Share Folder to get started. If you don't see the Share button, click the More Toolbar Items button ≫ at the end of the toolbar.

To see all your documents stored in iCloud Drive, click the iCloud Drive folder in the sidebar. To see only the documents that you're sharing, that are shared with you, and that you've been invited to collaborate on, click the Shared folder. To change what's shown in the sidebar, choose Finder > Settings.

Sync information between your Mac and other devices

You can connect your iPhone, iPad, or iPod touch to your Mac to transfer and update items between devices.

For example, when you add a movie to your Mac, you can sync with your iPhone and watch the movie on both devices.

You can sync items including music, movies, TV shows, podcasts, books, and more.

Use keyboard shortcuts to quickly get things done

You can use keyboard shortcuts to quickly perform common actions.

Mac basics

Connect to the internet

You can connect to the internet from your Mac, whether you're at home, at work, or on the go. Two common ways to get online are by using a Wi-Fi (wireless) or Ethernet (wired) connection. If neither is available, you may be able to use an Instant Hotspot.

Use Wi-Fi

When a Wi-Fi network is available, the Wi-Fi icon 📶 is shown in the menu bar at the top of the screen. Click the icon, then choose a network to join. If a lock icon 🔒 is shown next to the network name, the network is protected by a password—you need to enter the password before you can use that Wi-Fi network.

Use Ethernet

You can use Ethernet either through an Ethernet network or through a DSL or cable modem. If Ethernet is available, connect an Ethernet cable to the Ethernet port on your Mac, identified by this symbol ⟨•••⟩. If your Mac doesn't include a built-in Ethernet port, you can use an adapter to connect the Ethernet cable to the USB or Thunderbolt port on your computer.

Use Instant Hotspot

If you don't have access to a Wi-Fi or Ethernet connection, you may be able to use your Mac and Instant Hotspot to connect to the internet using the personal hotspot on your iPhone or iPad.

At home, at work, or on the go

When you're at home: Your ISP may offer a Wi-Fi or Ethernet internet connection. Check with your ISP if you're not sure which type of access you have.

When you're at work: You may have a Wi-Fi or Ethernet network connection available. Check with your company's IT department or network administrator for details about how to connect to your work network, and usage policies.

When you're on the go: You can use Wi-Fi hotspots (wireless networks that are open to the public) or Instant Hotspot on your Mac (if your Mac and your phone carrier support it). Keep in mind that some Wi-Fi hotspots require that you enter a password, agree to terms of service, or pay a fee to use it.

Browse the web

Use Safari on your Mac to browse websites and find almost anything on the web. Here's how to get started.

Search for information

You can use the Smart Search field at the top of the Safari window to search the web for almost anything. Enter what you're looking for—like "ice cream near me"—then click one of the search suggestions that appear.

Go to a website

You can also use the Smart Search field at the top of the Safari window to visit a website. Just enter its name or web address.

Choose a homepage

If you like to visit a website often, you can make it your homepage and have it appear whenever you open a new Safari window. Choose Safari > Settings, click General, then enter a webpage address (or click Set to Current Page to choose the webpage you're currently viewing).

Bookmark websites

When you find websites you want to go back to, you can bookmark them to easily revisit. Click the Share button ⬆️ in the toolbar, then choose Add Bookmark. To visit a bookmarked website, click the Sidebar button 🗔 in the toolbar, then click the Bookmarks button 🔖.

Take a screenshot

You can take pictures (called *screenshots*) or recordings of the screen on your Mac using Screenshot or keyboard shortcuts. Screenshot provides a panel of tools that let you easily take screenshots and screen recordings, with options to control what you capture—for example, you can set a timer delay or include the pointer or clicks.

Take pictures or screen recordings using Screenshot

1. On your Mac, press Shift-Command-5 (or use Launchpad) to open Screenshot and display the tools.

2. Click a tool to use to select what you want to capture or record (or use the Touch Bar).
   For a portion of the screen, drag the frame to reposition it or drag its edges to adjust the size of the area you want to capture or record.

Action	Tool
Capture the entire screen	
Capture a window	
Capture a portion of the screen	
Record the entire screen	
Record a portion of the screen	

Click Options if you want.

The available options vary based on whether you're taking a screenshot or a screen recording. For example, you can choose to set a timed delay or show the mouse pointer or clicks, and specify where to save the file.

The Show Floating Thumbnail option helps you work more easily with a completed shot or recording—it floats in the bottom-right corner of the screen for a few seconds so you have time to drag it into a document, mark it up, or share it before it's saved to the location you specified.

3.   Start the screenshot or screen recording:
    ○ *For the entire screen or a portion of it:* Click Capture.
    ○ *For a window:* Move the pointer to the window, then click the window.
    ○ *For recordings:* Click Record. To stop recording, click the Stop Recording button ⏹ in the menu bar.
4.   When the Show Floating Thumbnail option is set, you can do any of the following while the thumbnail is briefly displayed in the bottom-right corner of the screen:
    ○ Swipe right to immediately save the file and make it disappear.
    ○ Drag the thumbnail into a document, an email, a note, or a Finder window.
    ○ Click the thumbnail to open a window where you can mark up the screenshot or trim the recording, or share it.
5.   Depending on where you chose to save the screenshot or recording, an app may open.

Take pictures using keyboard shortcuts

You can use various keyboard shortcuts on your Mac to take pictures of the screen. The files are saved to the desktop.

Tip: To copy a screenshot so you can paste it somewhere—like in an email or to another device—press and hold the Control key while you press the other keys. For example, to copy the whole screen, press Shift-Command-Control-3.

Action	Shortcut

Capture the entire screen	Press Shift-Command-3.
Capture a portion of the screen	Press Shift-Command-4, then move the crosshair pointer to where you want to start the screenshot. Press the mouse or trackpad button, drag over the area you want to capture, then release the mouse or trackpad button.
Capture a window or the menu bar	Press Shift-Command-4, then press the Space bar. Move the camera pointer over the window or the menu bar to highlight it, then click.
Capture a menu and menu items	Open the menu, press Shift-Command-4, then drag the pointer over the menu items you want to capture.
Open Screenshot	Press Shift-Command 5.
Capture the Touch Bar	Press Shift-Command-6.

You can customize these keyboard shortcuts in Keyboard settings. On your Mac, choose Apple menu > System Settings, click Keyboard ⌨ in the sidebar, click Keyboard Shortcuts on the right, then click Screenshots. (You may need to scroll down.)

Screenshots are saved as .png files and screen recordings are saved as .mov files. Filenames begin with "Screenshot" or "Screen Recording" and include the date and time.

You may not be able to take pictures of windows in some apps, such as DVD Player.

Change your display's brightness

You can adjust the display's brightness manually or automatically.

Use the brightness function keys

If the screen seems too light or too dark, you can adjust your display's brightness.

- On your Mac, press the increase brightness key ☼ or the decrease brightness key ☼ (or use the Control Strip).

Automatically adjust brightness

1. If your Mac has an ambient light sensor, choose Apple menu > System Settings, then click Displays ☼ in the sidebar. (You may need to scroll down.)
2. Turn on "Automatically adjust brightness" on the right.

If you don't see the "Automatically adjust brightness" option, you can manually adjust the brightness.

Manually adjust brightness

1. On your Mac, choose Apple menu > System Settings, then click Displays ☼ in the sidebar. (You may need to scroll down.)
2. Drag the Brightness slider on the right to adjust the brightness of your display.

Depending on the type of display connected to your Mac, you may also see a Contrast slider that you can use to adjust the display's contrast.

For specific information about the brightness of your display, check the documentation that came with your display.

Adjust the volume

To change the volume on your Mac, do any of the following:

- Use the volume keys on your keyboard or use the Control Strip. For example, to quickly mute the volume, press ◀.

- Click the Sound control ◀))) in the menu bar or Control Center, then drag the slider to adjust the volume.
  Note: If the Sound control isn't in the menu bar, choose Apple menu > System Settings, then click Control Center in the sidebar. (You may need to scroll down.) Click the pop-up menu next to Sound on the right, then choose whether to show Sound in the menu bar all the time or only when it's active.

- Use the volume controls within apps, like the Apple TV app.

Use trackpad and mouse gestures

When you use an Apple trackpad or a Magic Mouse with your Mac, you can use gestures—such as click, tap, pinch, and swipe—to zoom in on documents, browse through music or webpages, rotate photos, open Notification Center, and more.

Trackpad gestures

Use one or more fingers on the surface of your trackpad to click, tap, slide, swipe, and more. For example, to move between pages of a document, swipe left or right with two fingers.

- To view the trackpad gestures you can use on your Mac, and a brief video demonstrating each gesture, choose Apple menu > System Settings, then click Trackpad in the

sidebar. (You may need to scroll down.)
You can also turn off or customize gestures in Trackpad settings.

Mouse gestures

Use one or more fingers on the surface of your mouse to click, tap, slide, or swipe items. For example, to move between pages of a document, swipe left or right with one finger.

- To view the mouse gestures you can use on your Mac, and a brief video demonstrating each gesture, choose Apple menu > System Settings, then click Mouse in the sidebar. (You may need to scroll down.)
  You can also turn off or customize gestures in Mouse settings.

Use Touch ID

If your Mac or Magic Keyboard has Touch ID, you can use it to unlock your Mac, authorize purchases from the iTunes Store, the App Store, and Apple Books, and make purchases on the web using Apple Pay. You can also use Touch ID to sign into some third-party apps.

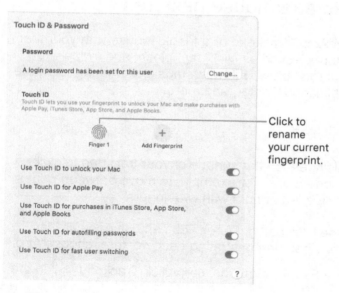

Click to rename your current fingerprint.

Set up Touch ID

1. On your Mac, choose Apple menu > System Settings, then click Touch ID & Password in the sidebar. (You may need to scroll down.)
2. Click Add Fingerprint, enter your password, then follow the onscreen instructions.
   If your Mac or Magic Keyboard has Touch ID, the sensor is located at the top right of your keyboard. You can add up to three fingerprints to your user account (you can save up to five fingerprints on your Mac).

Touch ID

3. Choose how you want to use Touch ID:
   - *Unlock your Mac:* Use Touch ID to unlock this Mac when you wake it from sleep.
   - *Apple Pay:* Use Touch ID to complete purchases you make on this Mac using Apple Pay.
   - *iTunes Store, App Store, and Apple Books:* Use Touch ID to complete purchases you make on this Mac from the Apple online stores.
   - *Autofill passwords:* Use Touch ID to automatically fill in user names and passwords and to automatically fill in credit card information when requested while using Safari and other apps.
   - *Fast user switching:* Use Touch ID to switch between user accounts on this Mac.

Rename or delete fingerprints

1. On your Mac, choose Apple menu > System Settings, then click Touch ID & Password   in the sidebar. (You may need to scroll down.)
2. Do any of the following:
   - *Rename a fingerprint:* Click the text below a fingerprint, then enter a name.
   - *Delete a fingerprint:* Click a fingerprint, enter your password, click Unlock, then click Delete.

Use Touch ID to unlock your Mac, log in, or switch users

To use Touch ID for these tasks, you must have logged in to your Mac already by entering your password.

- *Unlock your Mac and some password-protected items:* When you wake your Mac from sleep, or open a password-protected item, just place your finger on Touch ID when asked.
- *Log in from the login window:* Click your name in the login window, then place your finger on Touch ID.
  Only user accounts that have passwords can be unlocked with Touch ID. Sharing-only users and guest users cannot use Touch ID.

- *Switch users:* Click the fast user switching menu in the menu bar, choose a different user, then place your finger on Touch ID.
  To use Touch ID to switch to another user, you need to have set up fast user switching, and the user you switch to must have logged in to the Mac already by entering a password.

Use Touch ID to purchase items

1. Log in to your Mac by entering your password.
2. Purchase items using Apple Pay or from one of the online Apple stores.
3. Place your finger on Touch ID when asked.

If you have problems with Touch ID

- *If Touch ID doesn't recognize your fingerprint:* Make sure your finger is clean and dry, then try again. Moisture, lotions, cuts, or dry skin can affect fingerprint recognition.
- *If you have a Magic Keyboard with Touch ID:* If you can't unlock your Mac, enroll a fingerprint, or enter your password using Touch ID.
- *If you still have to enter your password:* For security, you need to enter your password when you start your Mac. Sometimes you need to enter your password to continue using Touch ID. For example, users must re-enter their password every 48 hours and after five incorrect fingerprint attempts.

Note: For added security, only logged-in users can access their own Touch ID information; an administrator cannot change another user's Touch ID settings or fingerprints.

Print documents

Use the Print dialog on your Mac to select a printer and set print options that determine how an image or document appears on the printed page.

1. With a document open on your Mac, choose File > Print, or press Command-P.
   The Print dialog opens, with a preview of your printed document.
   Note: You might see different options in the Print dialog depending on your printer and the app you're using. If the following steps differ from what you're seeing, check the documentation for the app you're using by clicking Help in the menu bar.

Tip: To view a full-size preview in the Preview app, click the PDF pop-up menu, then choose Open PDF in Preview.

2. If the settings in the Print dialog are fine as is, click Print, and you're done. Otherwise, continue to step 3.

3. To adjust the printing options, choose any of the following common print settings:

   o *Printer:* Choose the printer you want to use. If the printer isn't available, you can add one.

   o *Presets:* Choose a preset for the printer to use with your document, A preset is a group of print settings. In most cases you can use the default settings, but you can also choose a group of settings you've saved from a previous print job.

   o *Copies:* Specify the number of copies you want. To print all pages of a document before the next copy prints, click Paper Handling, then select "Collate Sheets."

   o *Print Range:* Specify the pages you want to print. You can print all pages or select a range of pages. For example, you can print page 6 through 9 of a 10-page document. You can also print a selection of pages in the range using the Selection button. Click the page label in the Preview sidebar to select the page for printing. Pages in your selection don't have to be in a continuous range. For example, you can

select to print page 2 and page 4 in a 5-page
document.

- o *Print in Color:* Select to print in color, if your printer
  has this capability. Turning the option off prints
  documents in black and white.
- o *Double-Sided:* Choose On from the Double-Sided
  pop-up menu to print on both sides of the paper (also
  called *duplexing* or two-sided printing), if your printer
  has this capability. You can also choose On (Short
  Edge) to set the document to print ready for binding
  at the top of the page.
- o *Paper Size:* Choose a paper size for your document.
  For example, choose US Letter when the printer is
  loaded with 8.5-by-11-inch paper.
- o *Orientation:* Click the buttons to switch between
  portrait or landscape orientation. The change in your
  document appears in the preview pages in the
  sidebar.
- o *Scaling:* Enter a percentage of scaling to adjust the
  printed image to the paper size. The change appears
  in the preview pages in the sidebar.

4. Click Print.

Keyboard shortcuts

You can use keystroke combinations, called *keyboard shortcuts,* to
perform tasks more quickly on your Mac. Keyboard shortcuts
include one or more modifier keys (such as Caps Lock or Control)
and a final key, pressed at the same time. For example, instead of
moving the pointer to the menu bar to choose File > New Window,
you can press the Command and N keys.

You can change or disable keyboard shortcuts to make them easier
to use.

Note: Keyboard shortcuts in apps may vary depending on the
language and keyboard layout you're using on your Mac. If the
shortcuts below don't work as you expect, look in the app menus in
the menu bar to see the correct shortcuts. You can also use the
Keyboard Viewer to see your current keyboard layout, known as an
input source.

Explore macOS keyboard shortcuts

Keyboard shortcuts appear next to menu items in macOS apps. Many keyboard shortcuts are standard across apps.

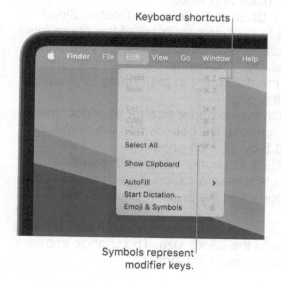

Keyboard shortcuts

Symbols represent modifier keys.

Perform tasks using keyboard shortcuts

- Press and hold one or more modifier keys (such as Caps Lock, Command, or Control), then press the last key of the shortcut.
  For example, to use the Command-V keyboard shortcut to paste copied text, press and hold the Command key at the same time as the V key, then release both keys.

Customize keyboard shortcuts

You can customize some keyboard shortcuts by changing the key combinations.

1. On your Mac, choose Apple menu > System Settings, click Keyboard in the sidebar (you may need to scroll down), then click Keyboard Shortcuts on the right.

2. In the list on the left, select a category, such as Mission Control or Spotlight.
   You can also customize keyboard shortcuts for specific apps by clicking the App Shortcuts category on the left.
3. In the list on the right, select the checkbox next to the shortcut that you want to change.
4. Double-click the current key combination, then press the new key combination you want to use.
   You can only use each type of key (for example, a letter key) once in a key combination.
5. Quit and reopen any apps you're using for the new keyboard shortcut to take effect.
   If you assign a keyboard shortcut that already exists for another command or app, your new shortcut won't work. You need to change your new shortcut or the other shortcut.
   To return all the shortcuts to their original key combinations, go to Keyboard settings, click Keyboard Shortcuts, then click Restore Defaults in the bottom-left corner.

Disable a keyboard shortcut

Sometimes an app's keyboard shortcut conflicts with a macOS keyboard shortcut. If this happens, you can disable the macOS keyboard shortcut.

1. On your Mac, choose Apple menu > System Settings, click Keyboard ⌨ in the sidebar (you may need to scroll down), then click Keyboard Shortcuts on the right.
2. In the list on the left, select a category, such as Mission Control or Spotlight.
3. In the list on the right, deselect the checkbox next to the shortcut that you want to disable.

Apps

Apps on your Mac

Your Mac comes with a wide range of apps already installed, so you can have fun, work, connect with friends, get organized, buy things, and more. To see the apps available on your Mac, click the

Launchpad icon ⚏ in the Dock. To open an app, click its icon in the Dock or use Launchpad.

Tip: Every app that comes with your Mac includes built-in help. To learn how to use an app, open the app, then choose Help in the menu bar. Or click a link below in the Description column to open the user guide for an app.

Apps

Note: Not all apps, services, features, or content are available in all countries or regions.

Icon	App	Description
	App Store	Find, buy, install, update, and review apps for Mac.
	Automator	Automate tasks without complicated programming or scripting languages.
	Books	Get and read classics and bestsellers, listen to audiobooks, or study textbooks.

	Calculator	Perform basic, advanced, or programmer calculations.
	Calendar	Track meetings, events, and appointments in one place.
	Chess	Play chess with your Mac or another player.
	Clock	Set alarms and timers, or use the world clock and stopwatch.
	Contacts	Store the phone numbers, addresses, birthdays, and more of people in your life.
	Dictionary	Look up words in dictionaries and other sources.
	FaceTime	Make video and audio calls.
	Find My	See the location of your friends, devices, and items.
	Font Book	Install, manage, and preview fonts.

	Freeform	Collaborate with others and bring ideas to life using Freeform boards.
	GarageBand	A fully equipped music creation studio right inside your Mac.
	Home	Control and automate HomeKit-enabled accessories.
	iMovie	Browse video clips, share favorite moments, and create trailers and movies.
	Keynote	Create presentations with images, media, charts, animations, and more.
	Mail	Manage all your emails in one place.
	Maps	Get directions, traffic conditions, and public transport details.
	Messages	Send text and audio messages.
	Music	Listen to your music library and discover new artists.

	News	Stay informed with news from leading sources, curated by editors and personalized for you.
	Notes	Jot down a quick thought—add a photo, video, URL, or table—for later.
	Numbers	Create spreadsheets with formulas, functions, interactive charts, and more.
	Pages	Create word-processing and page layout documents with formatted text, images, media, tables, and more.
	Photo Booth	Take fun photos or record videos.
	Photos	Import, view, and organize your photos and videos.
	Podcasts	Discover and subscribe to audio stories that entertain, inform, and inspire.
	Preview	View and edit PDFs and images, import images, and take pictures of the screen.

	Reminders	Create lists for to-dos, projects, groceries, and anything else you need to track.
	Safari	Browse and shop the web securely.
	Screenshot	Capture pictures or recordings of the screen on your Mac.
	Shortcuts	Use ready-made shortcuts or create your own to automate everyday tasks on your Mac and get them done more quickly.
	Stickies	Keep notes, lists, and pictures on the desktop.
	Stocks	Get market news and watch your favorite stocks and exchanges.
	TextEdit	Create and edit plain text, rich text, HTML, and other document types.
	TV	Watch your favorite shows and movies, and discover new ones.
	Voice Memos	Record, play, edit, and share audio recordings.

Icon	App	Description
	Weather	View current weather conditions in your location and other locations around the world.

Utilities

Icon	App	Description
	Activity Monitor	Get details about the processor, apps, disks, memory, and network activity on your Mac.
	Airport Utility	Set up and manage a Wi-Fi network and AirPort Base Station.
	Audio MIDI Setup	Set up audio and MIDI devices connected to your Mac.
	Bluetooth® File Exchange	Make short-range wireless connections between devices.
	Boot Camp Assistant	Use Windows on your Intel-based Mac.
	ColorSync Utility	Adjust the color profiles on your Mac.

47

	Console	View log messages to find details about problems with your Mac.
	Digital Color Meter	Find the color value of any color on the display.
	Disk Utility	Manage disks, disk images, and RAID sets.
	DVD Player	Play DVDs or DVD movie files.
	Grapher	Visualize and analyze implicit and explicit equations.
	Image Capture	Transfer and scan images, or take a picture.
	Keychain Access	Store passwords and account information.
	Migration Assistant	Transfer your information from a Mac, PC, or disk.
	Print Center	View and manage print jobs.

	QuickTime Player	Play video or audio files.
	Screen Sharing	View and control the screen of another Mac on your network.
	Script Editor	Create powerful scripts, tools, and even apps.
	System Information	Get details about your Mac, check its warranty, and learn how to free up space.
	Terminal	Access the complete UNIX operating system in macOS via the command line.
	VoiceOver Utility	Customize VoiceOver, the screen reader built into macOS.

You can change the look of the menu bar, desktop picture, Dock, and built-in apps by choosing a light or dark appearance in System Settings.

During downtime, or if you reach the time limit set for apps in Screen Time settings, app icons are dimmed and an hourglass icon ⧗ is shown.

Open apps

You can have multiple apps open at the same time on your Mac, and leave them open. This is especially useful for apps you return to frequently, such as Safari or Mail.

The quickest way to open an app on your Mac is to click the app's icon in the Dock.

Click an app icon
to open the app.

If the icon isn't in the Dock, there are other ways to open the app on your Mac:

- Click the Launchpad icon ▦ in the Dock, then click an app icon.

- Use Siri 🔘 to open an app for you. Say something like "Open Calculator."

- Click Spotlight 🔍 in the menu bar, enter an app's name in the search field, then press Return.

- If you recently used an app, choose Apple menu > Recent Items, then choose the app.

- Click the Finder icon 🙂 in the Dock, click Applications in the sidebar of the Finder window, then double-click the app.

Work with app windows

When you open an app or the Finder on your Mac, a window opens on the desktop. Only one app at a time is active; the name of the app (in bold) and the app menus are shown in the menu bar.

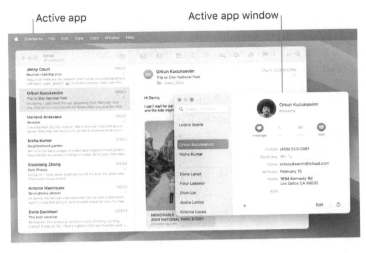

Active app | Active app window

Some apps, such as Safari or Mail, let you open multiple windows or different types of windows at the same time. There are several ways to manage open app windows on macOS, and close one or all of an app's windows.

Move, align, and merge app windows

On your Mac, do any of the following:

- *Manually move a window:* Drag the window by its title bar to where you want it. Some windows can't be moved.
- *Move a window to one side of the screen:* Press and hold the Option key while you move the pointer over the green

  button ⊕ in the top-left corner of the window, then choose Move Window to Left Side of Screen or Move Window to Right Side of Screen from the menu that appears. The window fills that half of the screen; the menu bar and Dock remain visible.
  To return the window to its previous position and size, press and hold the Option key, move the pointer over the green button, then choose Revert.
- *Align windows:* Drag a window close to another one—as the window nears the other one, it aligns without overlapping. You can position multiple windows adjacent to each other. To make adjacent windows the same size, drag the edge you want to resize—as it nears the edge of the adjacent window, it aligns with the edge and stops.

51

- *Merge an app's windows into one tabbed window:* In the app, choose Window > Merge All Windows. If an app has more than one type of window (such as Mail with the viewer window and the new message window), only the active type is merged.
  To make a tab a separate window again, select the tab, then choose Window > Move Tab to New Window, or just drag the tab out of the window.

Maximize or minimize app windows

On your Mac, do any of the following in a window:

- *Maximize a window:* Press and hold the Option key while you click the green button ⊕ in the top-left corner of an app window. To return to the previous window size, Option-click the button again.
  You can also double-click an app's title bar to maximize the window (as long as the option to do so is set to Zoom in Desktop & Dock settings).
- *Minimize a window:* Click the yellow minimize button ⊖ in the top-left corner of the window, or press Command-M.
  You can set an option in Desktop & Dock settings to have a window minimize when you double-click its title bar.

Most windows can be manually resized. Drag the window's edge (top, bottom, or sides) or double-click an edge to expand that side of the window.

Quickly switch between app windows

On your Mac, do any of the following:

- *Switch to the previous app:* Press Command-Tab.
- *Scroll through all open apps:* Press and hold the Command key, press the Tab key, then press the Left or Right arrow key until you get to the app you want. Release the Command key.
  If you change your mind while scrolling through the apps and don't want to switch apps, press Esc (Escape) or the Period key, then release the Command key.

Close one or all windows for an app

On your Mac, do any of the following:

- *Close a single window:* In a window, click the red Close button 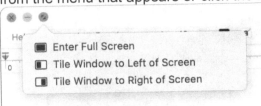 in the top-left corner of the window, or press Command-W.
- *Close all open windows for an app:* Press Option-Command-W.

Closing one or all windows for an app doesn't quit the app—it remains open (indicated by the small dot below the app's icon in the Dock). To quit the app, press Command-Q.

Use Mission Control to quickly arrange open windows and spaces in a single layer to easily spot the one you need.

Use apps in full screen

Many apps on your Mac support full-screen mode—an app fills the entire screen—so you can take advantage of every inch of the screen and work without desktop distractions.

1. On your Mac, move the pointer to the green button in the top-left corner of the window, then choose Enter Full Screen from the menu that appears or click the button .

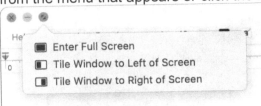

2. In full screen, do any of the following:
   - *Show or hide the menu bar:* Move the pointer to or away from the top of the screen. If you deselected the option to hide and show the menu bar in full screen, the menu bar is always shown.
   - *Show or hide the Dock:* Move the pointer to or away from the Dock's location.

- ○ *Move between other apps in full screen:* Swipe left or right on the trackpad with three or four fingers, depending on how you set your trackpad settings.
3. To stop using the app full screen, move the pointer to the green button again, then choose Exit Full Screen from the menu that appears or click the button .

To work in a bigger window without going full screen, you can maximize the window; the window expands, but the menu bar and the Dock remain visible.

If you're using an app full screen, you can quickly choose another app to use in Split View. Press Control-Up Arrow (or swipe up with three or four fingers) to enter Mission Control, drag a window from Mission Control onto the thumbnail of the full-screen app in the Spaces bar, then click the Split View thumbnail. You can also drag an app's thumbnail onto another in the Spaces bar.

Use apps in Split View

Many apps on your Mac support Split View, which lets you work in two apps side by side at the same time.

1. On your Mac, move the pointer to the green button in the top-left corner of the window, then choose Tile Window to Left of Screen or Tile Window to Right of Screen from the

menu that appears.

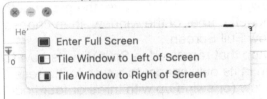

2. On the other side of the screen, click the second app you want to work with.
   The Split View is created in a new desktop space.
3. In Split View, do any of the following:
   - *Show or hide the menu bar:* Move the pointer to or away from the top of the screen. If you deselected the option to hide and show the menu bar in full screen, the menu bar is always shown.
   - *Show or hide the Dock:* Move the pointer to or away from the Dock's location.
   - *Show or hide a window's title and toolbar:* Click the window, then move the pointer to or away from the top of the screen.
   - *Make one side bigger:* Move the pointer over the separator bar located in the middle, then drag it left or right. To return to the original sizes, double-click the separator bar.
   - *Change sides:* Use a window's title and toolbar to drag the window to the other side.
   - *Use a different app on one side:* Click the app window, move the pointer over the green button in the top-left corner, choose Replace Tiled Window, then click the window you want to use instead. If you decide not to replace the current window, click the desktop to return to it.
   - *Move an app window to the desktop:* Click the app window, move the pointer over the green button in the top-left corner of the window, then choose Move Window to Desktop. The app is displayed on the desktop.
     The app that remained in Split View is now full screen in its own space; to return to it, press Control-Up Arrow (or swipe up with three or four fingers) to enter Mission Control, then click the app in the Spaces bar.

- *Use an app window full screen:* Click the app window, move the pointer over the green button in the top-left corner of the window, then choose Make Window Full Screen.
  The app that remained in Split View is now full screen in its own space; to return to it, press Control-Up Arrow (or swipe up with three or four fingers) to enter Mission Control, then click the app in the Spaces bar.

If you're using an app full screen, you can quickly choose another app to work with in Split View. Press Control-Up Arrow (or swipe up with three or four fingers) to enter Mission Control, drag a window from Mission Control onto the thumbnail of the full-screen app in the Spaces bar, then click the Split View thumbnail. You can also drag an app thumbnail onto another in the Spaces bar.

To use apps in Split View on other displays, make sure the "Displays have separate Spaces" option is turned on in Desktop & Dock settings.

Use Stage Manager

On your Mac, use Stage Manager to keep the app you're working with front and center, and your desktop clutter-free. Your recently used apps are neatly arranged along the left side of the screen for quick access, while the window you're working with is positioned in the center of the screen.

Arrange, resize, and overlap windows in your ideal layout. You can also arrange multiple apps on the screen to work together as a group in Stage Manager. When you switch to a group, all apps in the group open in the center of the screen.

Turn Stage Manager on or off

You can quickly move back and forth between Stage Manager and traditional windows to use the method that's best suited for the work you need to do.

On your Mac, do one of the following:

- On your Mac, choose Apple menu > System Settings, then click Desktop & Dock in the sidebar. (You may need to scroll down.) Go to Desktop & Stage Manager on the right, then turn Stage Manager on or off.
- Click Control Center in the menu bar, then click Stage Manager to turn it on or off.

Use Stage Manager

On your Mac, do any of the following:

- *Switch apps:* Click an app on the left side of the screen.
- *Arrange windows:* Reposition, resize, and overlap windows to suit your workflow.
- *Group apps:* Drag an app from the left side of the screen to add it to a group of apps in the center of the screen.

- *Ungroup apps:* Drag an app to the left side of the screen to remove it from the group.

If you turned off "Show recent apps in Stage Manager" in Stage Manager settings, the list of apps on the left is hidden. Move the pointer to the left edge of the screen to show it.

Show or hide Stage Manager in the menu bar

Stage Manager is always available in Control Center. You can choose to also show it in the menu bar.

1. On your Mac, choose Apple menu > System Settings, then click Control Center in the sidebar. (You may need to scroll down.)
2. Click the pop-up menu next to Stage Manager on the right, then choose Show in Menu Bar or Don't Show in Menu Bar.

Change Stage Manager settings

1. On your Mac, choose Apple menu > System Settings, then click Desktop & Dock in the sidebar. (You may need to scroll down.)
2. Go to Desktop & Stage Manager on the right.
3. Select or deselect the checkboxes next to Show Items:
    - *On Desktop:* Show desktop items.
    - *In Stage Manager:* Show desktop items when Stage Manager is turned on.
      If this option is turned off, items on the desktop are hidden—click the desktop to show the items when you want to access them.
4. Click the "Click wallpaper to reveal desktop" pop-up menu, then choose an option:
    - *Always:* Clicking the wallpaper moves all windows out of the way to show your desktop items and widgets.
    - *Only in Stage Manager:* When Stage Manager is turned on, clicking the wallpaper moves all windows

out of the way to show your desktop items and widgets.

5. Turn Stage Manager on or off.
6. Turn "Show recent apps in Stage Manager" on or off. If this option is turned off, recently used apps are hidden— move the pointer to the left edge of the screen to briefly show them.
7. Click the "Show windows from an application" pop-up menu, then choose an option:
    o   *All at Once:* Show all available windows for an app when you switch to it.
    o   *One at a Time:* Show only the most recently used window for an app when you switch to it. To switch to a different window when this option is turned off, click the app on the left again to open the next available window.

Get apps from the App Store

To find the perfect app or Safari extension, search for it or browse the App Store. After you find what you want, you can purchase it using your Apple ID, or you can redeem a download code or gift card.

Browse these areas for apps.

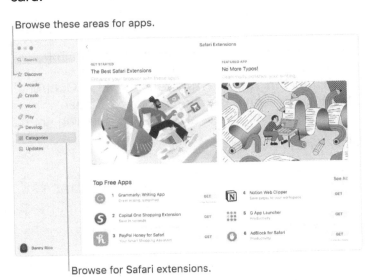

Browse for Safari extensions.

Find and buy apps

1. In the App Store 🅰 on your Mac, do any of the following:
   - *Search for an app:* Enter one or more words in the search field at the top-left corner of the App Store window, then press the Return key.
   - *Browse the App Store:* Click Discover, Create, Work, Play, Develop, or Categories in the sidebar on the left.
2. Apps shown with the Designed for iPhone or Designed for iPad label are also compatible with Mac computers with Apple silicon.
3. Click an app's name or icon to get a description, view customer ratings and reviews, and see the app's privacy practices.

Review how an app developer handles your data.

Data Not Collected
The developer does not collect any data from this app.

4. To download the app, click the button that shows the price of the app or "Get." Then click the button again to install or buy the app (or use Touch ID).
   To pause a download during installation, click the progress indicator ⏸. Click the Download button ⬇ to resume. You can also cancel a download before it has finished:
   - *From the Finder:* In the Applications folder, Control-click the app icon, then choose Move to Trash.
   - *From Launchpad:* Press and hold the app icon, then click ⊗.

Change your settings for downloads and purchases

1. On your Mac, choose Apple Menu > System Settings, then click [*your name*] at the top of the sidebar.
   If you don't see your name, click "Sign in with your Apple ID" to enter your Apple ID or to create one.
2. Click Media & Purchases.
3. Choose your options.

Redeem iTunes gift cards, Apple Music cards, or a download code

- In the App Store 🅰 on your Mac, click your name in the bottom-left corner (or click Sign In if you're not already), then click Redeem Gift Card in the top-right corner. Enter the download code or the code from your gift card.
  If you have a gift card with a box around the code, you can use the built-in camera on your Mac to redeem the card. After you click Redeem, click Use Camera, then hold the gift card 4 to 7 inches (10 to 18 centimeters) from the camera. Make sure the code area is near the center of the preview area, then hold the card steady until it's redeemed.

Purchase in-app content and subscriptions

- Some apps sell extra content, including app upgrades, game content, and subscriptions. To make an in-app purchase, enter your Apple ID (or use Touch ID).

Download apps purchased by other family members

If you're part of a Family Sharing group, you can download eligible apps purchased by other family members.

1. In the App Store 🅰 on your Mac, click your name in the bottom-left corner, or click Sign In if you're not already.
2. Click the "Purchased by" menu, then choose a family member.
3. Click the Download button ☁ next to an item.

To change your settings for downloads and purchases, choose Apple Menu > System Settings, click [your name] at the top of the sidebar, click Media & Purchases, then choose your options.

Install and reinstall apps from the App Store

There are several ways to install and reinstall apps that you purchased with your Apple ID.

61

Note: In the App Store, all of your purchases are tied to your Apple ID, and can't be transferred to another Apple ID. If you make purchases on your iPhone, iPad, or another Mac, always sign in using the same Apple ID so you can see all of your store purchases on this Mac and download any available updates.

Install apps that you purchased on a different device

You can install any app that you purchased with your Apple ID on another device.

1. In the App Store ![App Store icon] on your Mac, click your name in the bottom-left corner, or click Sign In if you're not already.
2. Locate the purchased app you want to download, then click

   the Download button ![Download icon].
   Tip: Hold the pointer over an active download's progress

   indicator ![indicator icon] to show the download speed and progress.

Automatically download apps that you purchased on a different device

1. In the App Store ![App Store icon] on your Mac, choose App Store > Settings.
2. Select "Automatically download apps purchased on other devices."

Reinstall apps

If you uninstalled or deleted an app that you purchased with your Apple ID, you can install it again.

1. In the App Store ![App Store icon] on your Mac, click your name in the bottom-left corner, or click Sign In if you're not already.
2. Locate the purchased app you want to reinstall, then click

   the Download button ![Download icon].

Install and uninstall other apps

You can download and install apps from the internet or a disc. If you no longer want an app, you can remove it.

Install apps

On your Mac, do any of the following:

- *For apps downloaded from the internet:* In the Downloads folder, double-click the disk image or package file (looks like an open box). If the provided installer doesn't open automatically, open it, then follow the onscreen instructions.
- *For apps on a disc:* Insert the disc into the optical drive on your Mac or connected to your Mac.

Uninstall apps

You can remove apps that you downloaded and installed from the internet or from a disc.

1. On your Mac, click the Finder icon in the Dock, then click Applications in the Finder sidebar.
2. Do one of the following:
   - *If an app is in a folder:* Open the app's folder to check for an Uninstaller. If Uninstall [*App*] or [*App*] Uninstaller is shown, double-click it, then follow the onscreen instructions.
   - *If an app isn't in a folder or doesn't have an Uninstaller:* Drag the app from the Applications folder to the Trash (at the end of the Dock).
   WARNING: The app is permanently removed from your Mac the next time you or the Finder empties the Trash. If you have files that you created with the app, you may not be able to open them again. If you decide you want to keep the app, get it back before emptying the Trash. Select the app in the Trash, then choose File > Put Back.

To uninstall apps you downloaded from the App Store, use Launchpad.

63

Files and folders

Create and work with documents

You can use macOS apps—such as Pages or TextEdit—or apps from the Mac App Store to create reports, essays, spreadsheets, financial charts, presentations, slideshows, and more.

Tip: If you have questions about how to use an app like Pages or TextEdit, choose Help in the menu bar while working in the app, then look for answers in the app's user guide.

Create documents

1. On your Mac, open an app that lets you create documents. For example, open TextEdit to create a plain text, rich text, or HTML document.
2. Click New Document in the Open dialog, or choose File > New.

Many Mac computers come with these Apple apps that you can use to create reports, spreadsheets, presentations, and more:

- *Pages:* Create letters, reports, flyers, posters, and more. Pages includes many templates that make it easy to create beautiful documents.
- *Numbers:* Create spreadsheets to organize and present your data. Start with a template, then modify it however you like— add formulas, charts, images, and more.
- *Keynote:* Create compelling presentations with images, media, charts, slide animations, and more.

If you don't have Pages, Numbers, or Keynote on your Mac, you can get them from the App Store.

They're also available for your iOS and iPadOS devices (from the App Store) and on iCloud.com.

Format documents

There are several ways to format and work with text in documents on your Mac:

- *Change fonts and styles:* In a document, choose Format > Show Fonts, Format > Font > Show Fonts, or Format > Style.
- *Change colors:* In a document, choose Format > Show Colors, or Format > Font > Show Colors.
- *Enter different types of characters:* You can enter characters with accent marks or diacritic marks.
- *Check spelling:* In most apps, spelling is checked while you type, and mistakes are automatically corrected. You can turn off these features or use other options.
- *Check definitions:* In a document, select the text you want to check, Control-click it, then choose Look Up.
- *Translate text:* In a document, select the text you want to translate, Control-click it, then choose Translate.

Save documents

Many apps on your Mac save your documents automatically while you work. You can save a document at any time.

- *Save a document:* In a document, choose File > Save, enter a name, choose where to save the document (to show more locations, click the down arrow button 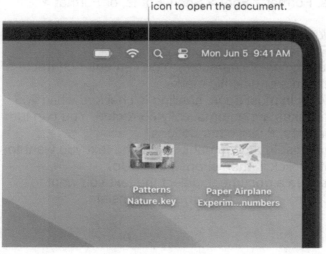), then click Save. When you save your document, you can add tags to it so it's easier to find later. You may be able to save your document in iCloud Drive so it's available on your computers and iOS and iPadOS devices set up with iCloud Drive.

- *Save a document with another name:* In a document, choose File > Save As, then enter a new name. If Save As isn't shown, press and hold the Option key, then open the File menu again.
- *Save a document as a copy:* In a document, choose File > Duplicate or File > Save As.

You can also save a document as a PDF and combine multiple files into a single PDF.

Open documents

The quickest way to open a document on your Mac is to double-click its icon on the desktop.

Double-click a document's
icon to open the document.

🔋 📶 Q 🖥 Mon Jun 5 9:41 AM

Patterns
Nature.key

Paper Airplane
Experim...numbers

If a document's icon isn't on the desktop, there are other ways to open the document on your Mac:

- Click Spotlight 🔍 in the menu bar, enter a document's name in the search field, then double-click the document in the results.
- If you recently worked in a document, choose Apple menu > Recent Items, then choose the document.
- Open the document's associated app, then choose the document in the Open dialog (if available), or choose File > Open. In some apps, you can choose File > Open Recent to open documents you have recently used.
- Click the Finder icon 🙂 in the Dock. In the Finder sidebar, click Recents, iCloud Drive, Documents, or the folder where the document is located, then double-click the document's icon or name.
  Note: Before you can open documents in iCloud Drive, you must set up iCloud Drive.

Tip: You can open files created with Microsoft Office on your Mac. Use the Pages app to open Microsoft Word documents, the Numbers app to open Microsoft Excel spreadsheets, and the Keynote app to open Microsoft PowerPoint presentations. If you don't have Pages, Numbers, or Keynote on your Mac, you can get them from the App Store.

Mark up files

Markup on your Mac lets you write, sign, and draw on, or crop or rotate, PDF documents and images. If your iPhone or iPad is nearby, you can use Continuity Markup to mark up the file on your device—even using Apple Pencil on iPad—and instantly show the changes on your Mac.

To use Continuity features, your devices must have Wi-Fi and Bluetooth® turned on, and meet system requirements.

1. When using Quick Look on your Mac, click the Markup tool Ⓐ. Or when using Quick Actions, choose Markup. Markup is also available in various apps, such as Mail, Notes, TextEdit, and Photos.
2. Use the tools listed below to mark up an image or a PDF document on your Mac.

The tools that are available vary depending on the type of file. If your iPhone or iPad is nearby, you can use Continuity Markup on your device to annotate a file.

If you don't like your changes, click Revert to remove them, then try again.

Tip: To duplicate any shape, text, or signature, press and hold the Option key while you drag an item; use the yellow guides to align the items. If you don't like your changes and want to start over, click Revert.

Tool	Description

Sketch	Sketch a shape using a single stroke. If your drawing is recognized as a standard shape, it's replaced by that shape; to use your drawing instead, choose it from the palette that's shown.
Draw	Draw a shape using a single stroke. Press your finger more firmly on the trackpad to draw with a heavier, darker line. This tool appears only on computers with a Force Touch trackpad.
Shapes	Click a shape, then drag it where you want. To resize the shape, use the blue handles. If it has green handles, use them to alter the shape. You can zoom and highlight shapes using these tools: • *Loupe*: Drag the loupe to the area you want to magnify. To increase or decrease the magnification, drag the green handle; drag the blue handle to change the loupe size. To further magnify an area, you can create additional loupes and stack them, using the yellow guides to align them. • *Highlight*: Drag the highlight where you want. To resize it, use the blue handles.
Text	Type your text, then drag the text box where you want.
Highlight Selection	Highlight selected text.

69

Sign	If signatures are listed, click one, then drag it where you want. To resize it, use the blue handles.
	To create a new signature, click the Sign tool, click Create Signature if shown, then click how you want to create your signature:
	• *Use a trackpad:* Click Trackpad, click the text when asked, sign your name on the trackpad using your finger, press any key when you're finished, then click Done. If you don't like the results, click Clear, then try again.
	If your trackpad supports it, press your finger more firmly on the trackpad to sign with a heavier, darker line.
	• *Use your Mac computer's built-in camera:* Click Camera, hold your signature (on white paper) facing the camera so that your signature is level with the blue line in the window. When your signature appears in the window, click Done. If you don't like the results, click Clear, then try again.
	• *Use your iPhone or iPad:* Click Select Device to choose a device (if more than one is available). On your device, use your finger or Apple Pencil (on iPad) to sign your name. If you don't like the results, tap Clear, then try again. When you're ready, tap Done.
	If you use VoiceOver, you can add a description of a signature when you create one. This is especially useful if you create multiple signatures and need to distinguish between them to ensure you use the intended signature. Before you click or tap Done, click the

	Description pop-up menu, then choose a description, such as Initials, or choose Custom to create your own description. When you're ready to sign a PDF document, navigate the list of signatures using VoiceOver. When you hear the description of the signature you want to use, press VO-Space bar. If you use iCloud Drive, your signatures are available on your other Mac computers that have iCloud Drive turned on.
Shape Style	Change the thickness and type of lines used in a shape, and add a shadow.
Border Color	Change the color of the lines used in a shape.
Fill Color	Change the color that's used inside a shape.
Text Style Aa	Change the font or the font style and color.
Rotate Left or Rotate Right	Click to rotate the item to the left. Continue clicking to keep rotating. To rotate the item to the right, press and hold the Option key, then click until you're done rotating the item.
Crop	Hide part of an item. Drag the corner handles until just the area you want to keep is shown within the frame's border. You can also drag the frame to reposition it. When you're ready, click Crop.
Image Description	Enter, view, or edit a description of an image. (The tool is highlighted when an image has a description.)

	Image descriptions can be read by screen readers and are useful for anyone who has difficulty seeing images online. For example, if you use VoiceOver, you can press the VoiceOver command VO-Shift-L to hear a description of the image in the VoiceOver cursor.
Annotate ▢, ▢, ⒶⒸ (Continuity Markup)	Annotate the item by sketching or drawing on it using your nearby iPhone ▢ or iPad ▢. If both devices are nearby, click Annotate ⒶⒸ, then choose a device. The tool may appear highlighted to show your device is connected. To disconnect your device without using it, click the tool again. When you annotate items on your iPad, you can use Apple Pencil. To switch between your markup and the iPad Home Screen, swipe up from the bottom of your iPad with one finger. To return to your markup, swipe up from the bottom with one finger to show the iPad Dock, then tap the Sidecar icon ▭. When you're done with the markup, tap Done.

When you're finished, click Done.
If you're working in the Quick Look or Quick Actions window, your changes can't be undone after you close the window.

Combine files into a PDF

You can quickly combine multiple files into a PDF right from your desktop or a Finder window.

1. On your Mac, click the Finder icon 🙂 in the Dock to open a Finder window.
2. Select the files you want to combine into a PDF. Alternatively, you can select the files on your desktop.

Note: The files appear in the PDF in the same order that you select them.

3. Control-click the selected files, then choose Quick Actions > Create PDF.

Select the files you want to combine.

Control-click one of the selected files for the Quick Actions menu.

The file is created automatically with a name similar to the first file you selected.

Tip: You can also select the files in the Finder and use the Create PDF button in the Preview pane of a Finder window. If you don't see the Preview pane on the right, choose View > Show Preview.

Organize files on your desktop

Desktop stacks on your Mac neatly organize files on your desktop into groups. When you save a file to the desktop, it's automatically added to the appropriate stack.

Turn on desktop stacks

- On your Mac, click the desktop, then choose View > Use Stacks or press Control-Command-0. You can also Control-click the desktop, then choose Use Stacks.

Browse files in a desktop stack

- On your Mac, swipe left or right on the stack using two fingers on the trackpad, or one finger on a Magic Mouse.

Expand or collapse a desktop stack

On your Mac, do any of the following:

- *Expand a stack:* Click it on the desktop. When the stack's expanded, double-click any item to open it.
- *Collapse a stack:* Click its Down Arrow icon.

Change how desktop stacks are grouped

You can group stacks by kind (such as images or PDFs), date (such as the date a file was last opened or created), or Finder tags.

- On your Mac, click the desktop, choose View > Group Stacks By, then choose an option. Or Control-click the desktop, choose Group Stacks By, then choose an option.

Change the appearance of desktop stacks

You can make icons bigger, change the spacing between icons, move icon labels to the side, or show more information (such as how many files are in a stack).

- On your Mac, click the desktop, choose View > Show View Options, then change options. Or Control-click the desktop, choose Show View Options, then change options.

You can display folders in the Dock as stacks.

Organize files with folders

Everything on your Mac—documents, pictures, music, apps, and more—is organized in folders. As you create documents, install apps, and do other work, you can create new folders to keep yourself organized.

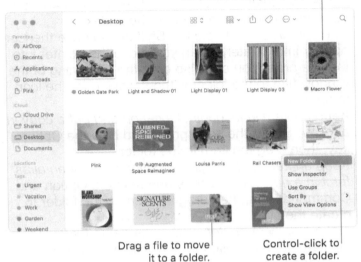

Hold the Option key and drag a
file to add a copy to a folder.

Drag a file to move
it to a folder.

Control-click to
create a folder.

Create a folder

1. On your Mac, click the Finder icon 😀 in the Dock to open a
   Finder window, then navigate to where you want to create
   the folder.
   Alternatively, click the desktop if you want to create the
   folder on the desktop.
2. Choose File > New Folder, or press Shift-Command-N.
   If the New Folder command is dimmed, you can't create a
   folder in the current location.
3. Enter a name for the folder, then press Return.

Move items into folders

1. On your Mac, click the Finder icon 😀 in the Dock to open a
   Finder window.
2. Do any of the following:
   - *Put an item in a folder:* Drag it to the folder.
   - *Put several items in a folder:* Select the items, then
     drag one of the items to the folder.
     All selected items move to the folder.

- Put a window's content in a folder: Move the pointer to the immediate left of the window title until an icon appears, then drag the icon to the folder.
  You can press and hold the Shift key to have the icon appear immediately when you move the pointer into the title area. You can also drag the beginning of the window title to the folder without waiting for the icon to appear.
- Keep an item in its original location and put a copy in a folder: Select the item, press and hold the Option key, then drag the item to the folder.
- Keep an item in its original location and put an alias for it in a new folder: Press and hold the Option and Command keys, then drag the item to the folder to create the alias.
- Make a copy of an item within the same folder: Select the item, then choose File > Duplicate or press Command-D.
- Copy files to a different disk: Drag the files to the disk.
- Move files to a different disk: Press and hold the Command key, then drag the files to the disk.

Quickly group multiple items into a new folder

You can quickly create a folder of items on the desktop or in a Finder window.

1. On your Mac, select all the items you want to group together.
2. Control-click one of the selected items, then choose New Folder with Selection.
3. Enter a name for the folder, then press Return.

Merge two folders with the same name

If you have two folders with identical names at two different locations, you can merge them into a single folder.

- On your Mac, press and hold the Option key, then drag one folder to the location that contains a folder with the same name. In the dialog that appears, click Merge.
  The Merge option appears only if one of the folders contains

items that are not in the other folder. If the folders contain different versions of identically named files, the only options are Stop or Replace.

To keep a handy list of files together that have something in common, based on criteria you specify, use a Smart Folder.

Tag files and folders

You can tag files and folders to make them easier to find. Tags work with all your files and folders, whether you store them on your Mac or keep them in iCloud.

Control-click a file or folder to select a tag.

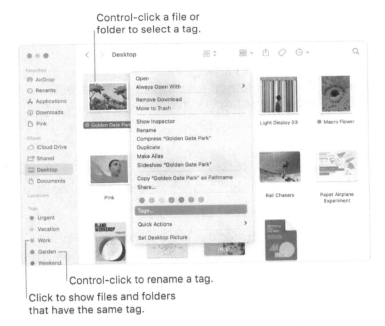

Control-click to rename a tag.
Click to show files and folders that have the same tag.

Tag files and folders

You can add multiple tags to any file or folder.

On your Mac, do any of the following:

- *Tag an open file:* Hold the pointer to the right of the document title, click the down arrow ⌄ , click in the Tags field, then enter a new tag, or choose one from the list.
- *Tag a new file when you save it:* Click File > Save. In the Save dialog, click in the Tags field, then enter a new tag, or choose one from the list.
- *Tag a file on the desktop or in the Finder:* Select the item, then open the File menu. You can also Control-click the item. Choose a color ○ above Tags (the name of the tag replaces Tags as you move the pointer over the color), or click Tags to choose from more tags or to enter a new tag. In a Finder window, you can also select the item, click the Tags button ♡ , then enter a new tag, or choose one from the list.

Tip: Use keyboard shortcuts to tag files quickly—select a file, then use Control-1 through Control-7 to add (or remove) your favorite tags. Control-0 (zero) removes all tags from a file.

Find items you tagged

1. On your Mac, click the Finder icon 🙂 in the Dock to open a Finder window.
2. Do any of the following:
   - *Search for a tag:* Enter the tag color or name in the search field, then select the tag from the suggestions.
   - *Select a tag in the sidebar:* To see everything with a certain tag, click the tag ○ in the Finder sidebar. To change the tags you see in the sidebar, choose Finder > Settings, click Tags, then select the tags you want to show.
   - *Group items by a tag:* Click the Group button ⊞, then choose Tags.
   - *Sort items by a tag:* In any view, choose View > Show View Options, click the Sort By pop-up menu, then choose Tags. In List view, select the Tags checkbox to display the column, move the pointer over the Tags column, then click it. Click the column name again to reverse the sort order.

Remove tags

On your Mac, do one of the following:

- *Remove tags from an item:* Control-click the item in a Finder window or on the desktop, then click Tags. Select the tags you want to remove, then press Delete.
- *Remove tags from your Mac:* In the Finder, choose Finder > Settings, then click Tags. Select the tags you want to remove, then click the Remove button ‾.

Edit tags

1. In the Finder 🔲 on your Mac, choose Finder > Settings, then click Tags.
2. Do any of the following:
   - *See a tag in the Finder sidebar:* Select the blue checkbox to the right of the tag.
   - *Change a tag color:* Click the color next to the tag ◯, then choose a new color.
   - *Change a tag name:* Click the tag, click the tag's name, then enter a new name.
   - *Create a new tag:* Click the Add button +.
   - *Delete a tag:* Select the tag, then click the Remove button ‾.
   - *Add a tag to the shortcut menu:* Select the tag in the list, then drag it over the tag you want to replace in the favorites section at the bottom of the window. There can be up to seven tags in the shortcut menu that appears when you Control-click a file.
   - *Remove a tag from the shortcut menu:* Drag the tag out of the Favorite Tags section until you see the remove sign ⊗.

Back up files

With Time Machine, you can back up files on your Mac that weren't part of the macOS installation, such as apps, music, photos, and documents. When Time Machine is turned on, it automatically backs up your Mac and performs hourly, daily, and weekly backups of your files.

When you use Time Machine, Time Machine also saves local snapshots you can use to recover previous versions of files, even if your backup disk is not attached. These snapshots are created hourly, stored on the same disk as the original files, and saved for up to 24 hours or until space is needed on the disk. Local snapshots are only created on disks using the Apple File System (APFS).

If you accidentally delete or change a file, you can use Time Machine to recover it.

Click arrows to navigate through backups.

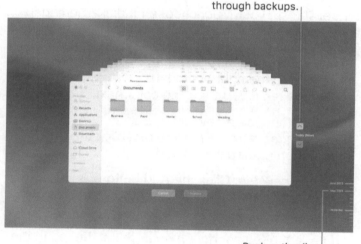

Backup timeline

Even though Time Machine creates local snapshots on computers using APFS, it's recommended that you back up your files to a location other than your internal disk, such as an external hard disk, a disk on your network, or a Time Capsule. That way, if anything ever happens to your internal disk or to your Mac, you can restore your entire system to another Mac.

1. Connect an external hard disk to your Mac and turn the disk on.
   Important: If you create a backup on a Mac running macOS Monterey or later, the files can only be restored to a Mac running Big Sur or later.

2. Do one of the following:
   - ○ *Set up a disk from the "Time Machine can back up your Mac" dialog:* If you don't currently have a Time Machine backup disk set up, you're asked if you want to use the disk to back up your Mac. Hold your pointer over the dialog that appears, click Options, then choose Set Up to use this disk as a backup disk with Time Machine. (If you choose Close, Time Machine closes, and the disk connects as a regular disk.)
   - ○ *Set up a disk in Time Machine Settings:* Click the Time Machine icon ⟲ in the menu bar, then choose Open Time Machine Settings.
     If the Time Machine icon isn't in the menu bar, choose Apple menu > System Settings. Click Control Center in the sidebar, scroll down to Time Machine 🕐, then select "Show in Menu Bar" from the pulldown menu.

3. Click Add Backup Disk or click the Add button ＋.
   The option you see depends on whether you have one or more backup disks already set up.

Important: Time Machine doesn't back up system files or apps installed during macOS installation.

Restore files

If you use Time Machine to back up the files on your Mac, you can easily get back lost items or recover older versions of files. You can use Time Machine within many apps by choosing File > Revert To > Browse All Versions.

1. On your Mac, open a window for the item you want to restore.
   For example, to recover a file you accidentally deleted from your Documents folder, open the Documents folder.
   If you're missing an item from the desktop, you don't need to open a window.

2. Use Launchpad to view and open apps on Mac and open Time Machine (in the Other folder). A message may appear while your Mac connects to the backup disk.
3. Use the arrows and timeline to browse the local snapshots and backups.

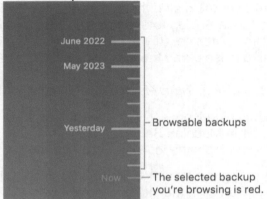

If you see a pulsing light to semi-dark gray tick mark, it represents a backup that's still loading or validating on the backup disk.
4. Select one or more items you want to restore (these can include folders or your entire disk), then click Restore. Restored items return to their original location. For example, if an item was in the Documents folder, it's returned to the Documents folder.

With many apps, you can use File > Revert To > Browse All Versions to view previous versions of documents in Time Machine, then find and restore the version you want.

Customize your Mac

Change System Settings

You can change system settings to customize your Mac. For example, you can choose a light or dark appearance, change the wallpaper, and more.

Choose options on the right.

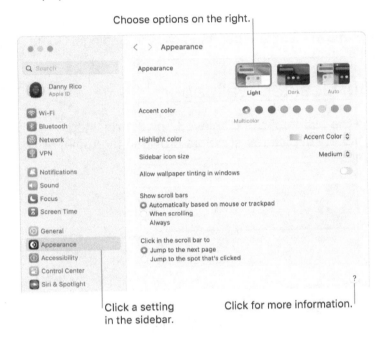

Click a setting in the sidebar.

Click for more information.

Options for your Mac are organized into settings. For example, options you can set for Accent color and Highlight color are located in Appearance settings.

1. Click the System Settings icon in the Dock or choose Apple menu > System Settings.
2. Click a setting.
   Settings are listed in the sidebar and may vary depending on your Mac and the apps you've installed.
3. Change an option.

Most settings include a Help button ⑦ to click for more information about the options.

If a red badge is shown on the System Settings icon in the Dock, you need to take one or more actions. For example, if you didn't fully set up iCloud features, the badge appears on the icon in the Dock; when you click the icon, the settings are displayed so you can complete setup.

To change options for an app, such as Mail or Safari, open the app, click the app's name in the menu bar, then choose Settings. Some apps don't offer settings.

Choose your desktop wallpaper

You can change the picture that's displayed on your desktop. Choose from a variety of pictures or colors provided by Apple, or use your own images.

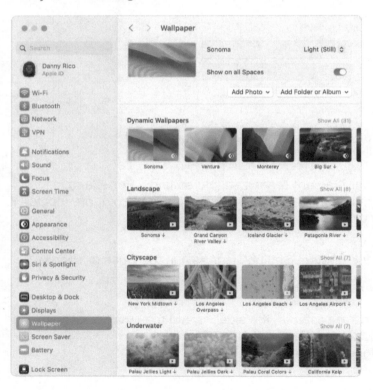

Tip: You can drag an image from your desktop or a folder onto the thumbnail of the current wallpaper to use the image as your wallpaper.

1. On your Mac, choose Apple menu > System Settings, then click Wallpaper in the sidebar. (You may need to scroll down.)
2. Select a wallpaper from one of the available categories:
   - *Add Photo/Add Folder or Album:* Controls to choose your own images.
   - *Dynamic Wallpapers:* These images brighten and darken, based on the time of day for your current location.
   - *Landscape, Cityscape, Underwater, and Earth aerials:* These still images show dramatic views.
   - *Shuffle Aerials:* These still images change at an interval you set.
   - *Pictures:* These still images show creative pictures.
   - *Colors:* These swatches apply a solid-color background for your desktop.
3. Set options for your wallpaper.
   Options vary based on the wallpaper you choose. For example, you can:
   - Turn on a slow-motion aerial as a screen saver, using the still aerial of your wallpaper.
   - Choose how often to shuffle through aerials.
   - Choose light or dark still versions of Dynamic Wallpaper.
   - Add your own color.

Tip: You can drag an image from your desktop or a folder onto the thumbnail at the top of Wallpaper settings to use the image as your wallpaper.

To quickly use a photo you have in the Photos app, open Photos, select the photo, click the Share button in the Photos toolbar, then choose Set Wallpaper.

You can also use a picture you find on the web as your wallpaper. Control-click the image in the browser window, then select Use Image as Desktop Picture.

Add and customize widgets

On your Mac, add widgets to the desktop or Notification Center so you can keep tabs on your schedule, favorite devices, the weather, top headlines, and more.

Drag widgets anywhere on the desktop.

Drag widgets to the upper-right corner of the desktop to add them to Notification Center.

Widget categories

To open Notification Center, click the date and time in the menu bar or swipe left with two fingers from the right edge of the trackpad. To close it, click anywhere on the desktop.

Tip: If your desktop widgets are hidden by other windows, click the wallpaper to move the open windows away so you can see the widgets.

If you don't want the open windows to move away when you click the desktop, you can change the setting "Click wallpaper to reveal desktop" in Desktop & Dock settings. Then clicking the desktop only moves the windows away when you're using Stage Manager.

Add widgets to the desktop

1. On your Mac, Control-click the wallpaper, then choose Edit Widgets.

2. In the widget browser, search for a widget. Or click a category, such as Clock, to view its available widgets.
3. To add widgets to the desktop, do any of the following:
   o *Automatically position a widget on the desktop:* Click the widget (or click the widget's Add button ⊕).
   o *Manually position a widget on the desktop:* Drag the widget to any position on the desktop.
4. To change the new widget's location, drag it to another location on the desktop. If you decide you don't want the new widget, click its Remove button ⊖ .
5. When you're finished adding widgets, click Done at the bottom-right corner of the widget browser.

Add widgets to Notification Center

1. On your Mac, open Notification Center.
2. At the bottom of Notification Center, click Edit Widgets.
3. In the widget browser, search for a widget. Or click a category, such as Clock, to view its available widgets.
4. To add widgets to Notification Center, do any of the following:
   o Drag the widget to the upper-right corner of the desktop.
   o Click the widget (or click the widget's Add button ⊕).
5. To change the new widget's location in Notification Center, drag it up or down. If you decide you don't want the new widget, click its Remove button ⊖ .
6. When you're finished adding widgets, click Done at the bottom-right corner of the widget browser.

Use iPhone widgets on your Mac

1. On your Mac, choose Apple menu > System Settings, then click Desktop & Dock ⬚ in the sidebar. (You may need to scroll down.)

2. Go to Widgets, then turn on "Use iPhone widgets."
   Your iPhone widgets are now available to add to the desktop or Notification Center from the widget browser.

Customize widgets

1. On your Mac, Control-click a widget.
2. Do any of the following:
   - *Change the information the widget shows:* Choose Edit [*widget name*], then change options or click highlighted information to change it. For example, in the List widget for Reminders, click the highlighted list to choose a different reminder list. When you're finished, click Done in the widget.
     Note: If Edit [*widget name*] isn't available in the shortcut menu, you can't change what the widget shows.
   - *Change the size of the widget:* Choose a different size.
   - *Remove the widget:* Choose Remove Widget.
3. When you're finished customizing widgets, click Done.

Remove widgets from the desktop

1. On your Mac, click the wallpaper, then choose Edit Widgets.
2. Click the Remove button ⊖ for the widget you want to remove.

Remove widgets from Notification Center

1. On your Mac, open Notification Center.
2. Do one of the following:
   - Control-click the widget you want to remove, then choose Remove Widget from the shortcut menu.
   - Move the pointer over the widget you want to remove, press and hold the Option key, then click the Remove button ⊖.

Change widget settings

1. On your Mac, choose Apple menu > System Settings, then click Desktop & Dock in the sidebar. (You may need to scroll down.)
2. Go to Widgets on the right.
3. Select or deselect the checkboxes next to "Show Widgets:"
    -   *On Desktop:* Show widgets on the desktop.
    -   *In Stage Manager:* Show widgets when Stage Manager is turned on.
        If this option is turned off, items on the desktop are hidden—click the desktop to show the items when you want to access them.
4. Click the "Widget style" pop-up menu, then choose an option:
    -   *Automatic:* Automatically switch between monochrome and full-color.
    -   *Monochrome:* Always show widgets in monochrome.
    -   *Full-color:* Always show widgets in full-color.
5. Turn "Use iPhone widgets" on or off.

Use a screen saver

You can use a screen saver to hide the desktop when you're away from your Mac or if you need extra privacy.

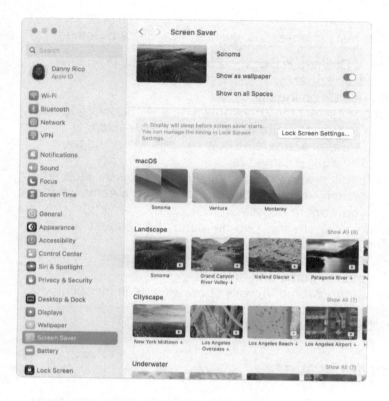

Customize the screen saver on your Mac

1. On your Mac, choose Apple menu > System Settings, then click Screen Saver in the sidebar. (You may need to scroll down.)
2. Select a screen saver from one of the available categories:
    o   *macOS:* These are slow-motion images.
    o   *Landscape, Cityscape, Underwater, and Earth aerials:* These slow-motion images show dramatic views.
    o   *Shuffle Aerials:* These slow-motion images change at an interval you set.
    o   *Other:* These distinctive screen savers allow you to show a message, see a "Word of the Day," and more.
3. Set options for your screen saver.
    Options vary based on the screen saver you choose. For example, you can:

- Turn on a still aerial for your wallpaper, using the slow-motion aerial of your screen saver.
- Choose how often to shuffle through aerials.
- Choose a style to shuffle through your images.

Start or stop the screen saver on your Mac

- The screen saver automatically starts whenever your Mac sits idle for the amount of time you choose. To change how long your Mac can be inactive before the screen saver starts, choose Apple menu > System Settings, then click Lock Screen in the sidebar. (You may need to scroll down.)
  If you set up a hot corner for the screen saver, move the pointer over the corner to immediately start the screen saver. You can also start the screen saver by choosing Apple menu > Lock Screen.
- To stop the screen saver and show the desktop, press any key, move the mouse, or touch the trackpad.

Add a user or group

If your Mac has multiple users, you should set up an account for each person so each can personalize settings and options without affecting the others. You can let occasional users log in as guests without access to other users' files or settings. You can also create groups that include the user accounts on your Mac. You must be an administrator of your Mac to perform these tasks.

Add a user

1. On your Mac, choose Apple menu > System Settings, then click Users & Groups in the sidebar. (You may need to scroll down.)
2. Click the Add User button below the list of users on the right (you may be asked to enter your password.)
3. Click the New User pop-up menu, then choose a type of user.

91

- *Administrator:* An administrator can add and manage other users, install apps, and change settings. The new user you create when you first set up your Mac is an administrator. Your Mac can have multiple administrators. You can create new ones, and convert standard users to administrators. Don't set up automatic login for an administrator. If you do, someone could simply restart your Mac and gain access with administrator privileges. To keep your Mac secure, don't share administrator names and passwords.
- *Standard:* Standard users are set up by an administrator. Standard users can install apps and change their own settings, but can't add other users or change other users' settings.
- *Sharing Only:* Sharing-only users can access shared files remotely, but can't log in to the computer or change settings.

4. For more information about the options for each type of user, click the Help button in the lower-left corner of the dialog. To give the user permission to access your shared files or screen, you may need to change options in File Sharing, Screen Sharing, or Remote Management settings.
5. Enter a full name for the new user. An account name is generated automatically. To use a different account name, enter it now—you can't change it later.
6. Enter a password for the user, then enter it again to verify. Enter a password hint to help the user remember their password.
7. Click Create User.
8. If you want, further refine what the user can do. Click the Info button ⓘ next to the user name, then do any of the following:
   - Select "Allow user to reset password using Apple ID." To use this option, the user must have set up iCloud on this Mac. However, this option isn't available for the Guest User account, or if FileVault is turned on and set to allow the user to reset their password at startup using their Apple ID.
   - To make a standard user an administrator, turn on "Allow user to administer this computer."

If your Mac or Magic Keyboard has Touch ID, a new user can add a fingerprint after logging in to the Mac.

Create a group

A group allows multiple users to have the same access privileges. For example, you can grant a group specific access privileges for a folder or a file, and all members of the group have access. You can also assign a group specific access privileges for each of your shared folders.

1. On your Mac, choose Apple menu > System Settings, then click Users & Groups in the sidebar. (You may need to scroll down.)
2. Click the Add Group button. (You may need to scroll down.)
3. Click the New Group pop-up menu, give the group a name, then click Create Group.
4. Click the Info button next to a group, then enable users in the list that appears.

To permit new users to share your files and share your screen, you may need to change options in File Sharing, Screen Sharing, or Remote Management settings.

Add your email and other accounts

You can use Exchange, Google, Yahoo, and other internet accounts in Mac apps by adding the accounts to your Mac.

You add internet accounts, and manage account settings, in Internet Accounts settings. You can also add internet accounts from some apps that use them.

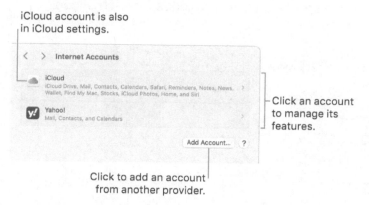

iCloud account is also in iCloud settings.

Click an account to manage its features.

Click to add an account from another provider.

An iCloud account you add using iCloud settings in Apple ID settings also appears in Internet Accounts settings. You can change its settings in either place.

Add an account from an app

You can add accounts directly from the Calendar, Contacts, and Mail apps. Accounts you add from these apps appear in Internet Accounts settings. Before you can add an account from an app, you must create the account on the provider's website.

1. In the app on your Mac, click the app's name in the menu bar, then choose Add Account.
   For example, in Mail, choose Mail > Add Account.
2. Select the account provider, then click Continue.
   If you want to add an account from a provider that isn't listed, such as a mail or calendar account for your company or school, select Other [Type of] Account, click Continue, then enter the requested account information. If you don't know the account information, ask the account provider.

3. Enter your account name, password, and other requested information.
4. If you're adding an account that multiple apps can use, a dialog appears in which you select the apps you want to use with the account.

Add an account in Internet Accounts settings

Before you can add an account in Internet Accounts settings, you must create the account on the provider's website.

1. On your Mac, choose Apple menu > System Settings, then click Internet Accounts @ in the sidebar. (You may need to scroll down.)
2. Click Add Account on the right, then click the name of an account provider.
   If you want to add an account from a provider that isn't listed, such as a mail or calendar account for your company or school, click Add Other Account, click the type of account you want to add, then enter the requested account information. If you don't know the type of account or the account information, ask the account provider.
3. Enter your account name, password, and other requested information.
4. If you're adding an account that multiple apps can use, a dialog appears in which you select the apps you want to use with the account.

Change account features and details

1. On your Mac, choose Apple menu > System Settings, then click Internet Accounts @ in the sidebar. (You may need to scroll down.)
2. Click an account on the right, then do one of the following:
   o *Turn features on or off:* Turn on or off any feature you want to use with the account.
   o *Change account details:* Click the Details button at the top. For some accounts, the account user name

or email, a description, and other details are already shown, and a Details button is not available.

Stop using an account

1. On your Mac, choose Apple menu > System Settings, then click Internet Accounts @ in the sidebar. (You may need to scroll down.)
2. Click the account you want to stop using on the right, then do one of the following:
   - *Remove the account and turn off its features:* Click Delete Account at the bottom, then click OK.
   - *Turn off a specific feature:* Click the switch next to the feature.
3. *Note:* Deleting an account or turning off individual features can remove data stored in your apps. The data may be restored if you turn on the feature or add the account again. If you're not sure, ask the account provider.

Automate tasks with Shortcuts

If you're looking for new shortcuts to add to your collection, or if you want to see what's possible and how particular shortcuts are built, check out the Gallery in the Shortcuts app.

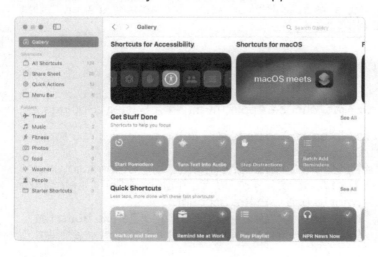

Open and browse the Gallery

1. In the Shortcuts app ![icon] on your Mac, click Gallery in the sidebar.
   Curated shortcuts appear organized into category rows (Essentials, Morning Routine, and so on).
2. To see all the shortcuts in a category, click See All.
3. Scroll a category row sideways to see other shortcuts in a category.
4. Scroll up or down to see more category rows.

Add a Gallery shortcut to your collection

1. In the Shortcuts app ![icon] on your Mac, click Gallery in the sidebar, then click a shortcut.
   A description of the shortcut appears.

   Tip: To quickly add a shortcut to your collection, click ![+] .
2. To see a preview of the actions in the shortcut, click the More button ![•••] .
   To return to the description, click Done.
3. To add the shortcut to your collection, click Add Shortcut.
4. If there are additional setup steps for the shortcut, follow the instructions that appear, then click Add Shortcut.
   The shortcut is added to your shortcuts collection.

Search the Gallery

You can search for additional shortcuts not shown in the Gallery.

- In the Shortcuts app ![icon] on your Mac, click Gallery in the sidebar, then enter a search term in the search field in the top-right corner.
  Shortcuts that match your search term appear below.

Create Memoji

With macOS 11 or later, you can create a personalized Memoji that matches your personality. Then, send Memoji to express your mood in your messages.

1. In the Messages app on your Mac, select any conversation.

2. Click the Apps button to the left of the text field, click the Stickers button , then select the Memoji button .

3. Click the Add button (for your first Memoji) or the More button , then follow the onscreen instructions to create and customize your Memoji, starting with skin tone all the way through clothing.

4. Click Done.

Change your login picture

You can change the picture that appears in the login window on your Mac. Your login picture is also displayed as your Apple ID picture and as your My Card in Contacts.

Note: You can't change the picture for another user that's currently logged in (indicated by a checkmark on the user's picture). The user must log in and change their picture or log out so you can change it.

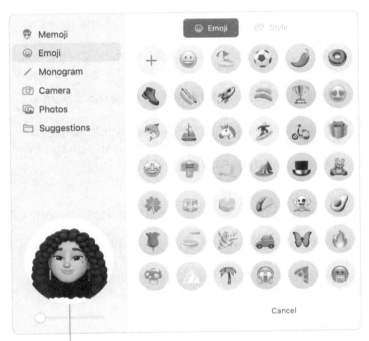

Click to change the user picture.

1. On your Mac, choose Apple menu > System Settings, then click Users & Groups in the sidebar. (You may need to scroll down.)
2. On the right, click the picture next to your login name, then do any of the following:
   - *Select a Memoji:* Click Memoji, then click the Add button to select and compose a facial image. Or select one of the displayed Memoji, then select a pose and style you like.
   - *Select an emoji:* Click Emoji, then click the Add button to select an image from the emoji library. Or select one of the displayed emoji and select a style.
   - *Select a monogram:* Click Monogram, select a background color, then enter initials.
   - *Take a picture using your Mac camera:* Click Camera. Set up your shot, then click the Camera

button. You can retake the photo as many times as you need to.

    ◦ *Select a photo from your Photos library:* Click Photos. To see photos from a specific album, click the arrow

      〉 next to Photos in the sidebar, click the album you want, then select a photo.

      Tip: To quickly replace the current Apple ID picture with an image on your Mac, just drag the image from the Finder onto the current picture.

    ◦ *Select a suggested image:* Click Suggestions, then select a picture.

3. After you select an image, you can adjust its look. Do any of the following:

    ◦ *Adjust the image location:* Drag the picture around within the circle.

    ◦ *Zoom in or out:* Drag the slider left or right.

4. Click Save.

Change the system language

Although your Mac is set to display the language of the country or region in which it was purchased, you can choose a different language to use. For example, if you bought your Mac in the United States but you work primarily in French, you can set your Mac to use French.

You can also choose different languages for individual apps. For example, if your system language is set to Simplified Chinese, but you prefer to use a certain app in English, you can do so.

Tip: If you're using a web browser like Safari to view this page, you can read it in another language. Scroll to the bottom of the page, click the name of the country or region in the bottom-right corner, then choose a country or region in the list.

Change the system language

1. On your Mac, choose Apple menu > System Settings (the second option in the menu), click General in the

sidebar, then click Language & Region ⊕ on the right. (You may need to scroll down.)

2. Under the Preferred Languages list at the top, do any of the following:

- *Add a language:* Click the Add button ╈ , select a language in the list, then click Add (the button in the bottom-right corner).
  The list is divided by a separator line. Languages above the line are system languages that are fully supported by macOS and are shown in menus, notifications, websites, and more. Languages below the line aren't fully supported by macOS, but may be supported by apps that you use, and on some websites.
  If you haven't already added an input source for typing in the language you're adding, a list of available input sources is shown. If you don't add an input source now, you can add it later in Keyboard settings.

- *Change the primary language:* Drag a language to the top of the languages list.
  Note: You may need to restart your Mac to see the change in all applications. Click Restart Now (the button on the right with red text) to restart your computer.
  If macOS, an app, or a website supports the primary language, the user interface is shown in that language. If the language isn't supported, the next language in the list is used, and so on.
  The order of the languages in the list determines how text appears when you type characters in a script that belongs to more than one language.

If your Mac has multiple users and you want everyone to see the language you chose as the primary language in the login window,

click the Settings pop-up menu ⚙, then choose Apply to Login Window. (If the Settings pop-up menu doesn't appear, it means the login window is already set to use the primary language.)

Choose the language you use for individual apps

1. On your Mac, choose Apple menu > System Settings, click General in the sidebar, then click Language & Region on the right. (You may need to scroll down.)
2. Go to Applications, then do any of the following:
   - *Choose a language for an app:* Click the Add button ┬, choose an app and a language from the pop-up menus, then click Add.
   - *Change the language for an app in the list:* Select the app, then choose a new language from the pop-up menu.
   - *Remove an app from the list:* Select the app, then click the Remove button ▬. The app uses the default language again.

If the app is open, you may need to close and then reopen it to see the change.

Make text and other items on the screen bigger

You can change the display resolution to make everything on the screen bigger, or increase the size of text and icons to make them easier to see.

Tip: If you have trouble finding the pointer on the screen, you can make it bigger too, or quickly locate it with a shake of your mouse.

Make everything on the screen bigger

You can adjust your display's resolution to make everything on the screen appear larger.

1. On your Mac, choose Apple menu > System Settings, then click Displays in the sidebar. (You may need to scroll down.)
2. On the right, select a resolution.
   A lower resolution increases the size of everything on the screen.

Make text and icons bigger across apps and system features

You can use a single slider to adjust the preferred reading size for text across multiple apps, as well as on the desktop and in sidebars.

1. On your Mac, choose Apple menu > System Settings, then click Accessibility in the sidebar. (You may need to scroll down.)
2. Click Display on the right, go to Text, then click "Text size." (You may need to scroll down.)
3. Drag the slider to the right to increase the text size on the desktop, in sidebars, and in the listed apps (if they are set to Use Preferred Reading Size).
   To set a different text size for any of the listed apps, click the pop-up menu next to the app, then choose a size.
   Note: If an app is set to Customized in App, a unique text size has been set in that app's settings. If you change the app's text size in System Settings, it replaces the text size customization you set in the app.

Tip: You can view a larger version of onscreen text when you move the pointer over it.

Make text bigger for individual apps or system features

In many apps, you can adjust the reading size for text in just that app. You can also adjust the text size in desktop labels and sidebars.

- *In apps:* In some apps, such as Mail, Messages, and News, you can press Command-Plus (+) or Command-Minus (−) to adjust the text size as you read emails, messages, and articles.
  You can also use System Settings to set a preferred reading size for text in individual apps, such as Calendar, Mail, and Messages.
- *In webpages:* In Safari, press Command-Option-Plus (+) or Command-Option-Minus (−) to adjust the text size.

- *In file and folder names in the Finder:* Choose View > Show View Options. Click the "Text size" pop-up menu, then choose a text size.
  Note: You can't change the text size in Gallery view.
- *In desktop labels:* Control-click the desktop, choose Show View Options, click the "Text size" pop-up menu, then choose a text size.

- *In sidebars:* Choose Apple menu > System Settings, then click Appearance 🔵 in the sidebar (you may need to scroll down). Click the pop-up menu next to "Sidebar icon size" on the right, then choose Large.

Make icons bigger for individual apps or system features

You can adjust the icon size for items in the Finder, on the desktop, or in sidebars.

- *In Finder windows:* Choose View > Show View Options. In Icon view and List view, choose a larger icon size. In Gallery view, you can choose a larger thumbnail size.
  Note: You can't change the icon size in Column view.
- *On the desktop:* Control-click the desktop, choose Show View Options, then drag the "Icon size" slider to the right.

- *In sidebars:* Choose Apple menu > System Settings, then click Appearance 🔵 in the sidebar (you may need to scroll down). Click the pop-up menu next to "Sidebar icon size" on the right, then choose Large.

You can also use your keyboard, mouse, or trackpad to quickly zoom in and out on what's onscreen.

Beyond Mac basics

Set up a Focus to stay on task

When you need to stay on task and minimize distractions, use Focus. You can use a Focus to pause and silence all notifications or allow only certain notifications—for example, ones from colleagues on an urgent project. You can also share that you've silenced notifications so contacts know you're busy.

Allow notifications from
certain people and apps.

Add a Focus filter.
Schedule a Focus.

Tip: Need to quickly silence all notifications? Turn on the Do Not Disturb Focus in Control Center.

Add or remove a Focus

1. On your Mac, choose Apple menu > System Settings, then click Focus in the sidebar. (You may need to scroll down.)
2. Do any of the following on the right:
   - *Add a provided Focus:* Click Add Focus, then click a Focus, such as Gaming or Work.
   - *Create a custom Focus:* Click Add Focus, then click Custom. Enter a name, select a color and icon, then click OK. For example, you might create a Study Focus. You can create up to ten.
   - *Remove a Focus:* Click a Focus in the list, then click Delete Focus at the bottom of the window.
     A custom Focus is deleted. A provided Focus, such as Reading or Mindfulness, is removed from the list but is still available to add again later.

If you keep Focus up to date across your Apple devices, the changes you make on your Mac are reflected on your other devices.

Choose which notifications to allow

You can specify which notifications are shown when a Focus is active—for example, notifications from certain people and apps, time-sensitive notifications, or notifications for phone calls received on your Mac.

Note: Some apps, such as Calendar, have time-sensitive notifications. To ensure you receive these notifications, select the option to allow them.

1. On your Mac, choose Apple menu > System Settings, then click Focus in the sidebar. (You may need to scroll down.)
2. Click a Focus on the right.
3. Go to Allow Notifications, click Allowed People, then do any of the following (click Done when you're finished):
   - *Allow notifications from certain people:* Click the pop-up menu next to Notifications, then choose Allow Some People. Click the Add People button , then

select one or more contacts. For example, for the Gaming Focus, you might select the friends you usually play with in multiplayer games.
To remove a person from the list, move the pointer over the person, then click the Remove button .

- ○ *Silence notifications from certain people:* Click the pop-up menu next to Notifications, then choose Silence Some People. Click the Add People button , then select one or more contacts.
  To remove a person from the list, move the pointer over the person, then click the Remove button .
- ○ *Allow notifications for phone calls:* Click the pop-up menu next to "Allow calls from," then choose an option. You can receive notifications for calls from everybody, allowed people only, only people in your contacts list in Contacts, or only people in your Favorites on iPhone.
- ○ *Allow notifications for repeated phone calls:* Turn on "Allow repeated calls" to receive notifications from anyone who calls two or more times within three minutes.

4. Go to Allow Notifications, click Allowed Apps, then do any of the following (click Done when you're finished):
   - ○ *Allow notifications from certain apps:* Click the Notifications pop-up menu, then choose Allow Some Apps. Click the Add button, select one or more apps, then click Add. For example, for the Work Focus, you might allow notifications only from the apps you need to do your work.
     To remove an app from the list, move the pointer over the app, then click the Remove button .
   - ○ *Silence notifications from certain apps:* Click the Notifications pop-up menu, then choose Silence Some Apps. Click the Add button, select one or more apps, then click Add.
     To remove an app from the list, move the pointer over the app, then click the Remove button .
   - ○ *Allow notifications for events or tasks that require your immediate attention:* Turn on "Time sensitive notifications." (Make sure you also select the option

107

that allows apps to send these notifications in Notifications settings.)

The Gaming Focus is set by default to turn on whenever a game controller is connected with your Mac. To receive notifications when the Gaming Focus is on, be sure to specify people or apps.

Schedule a Focus to turn on or off automatically

You can schedule a Focus to automatically turn on or off at certain times, when you arrive at or leave certain locations, or when you open or close certain apps.

1. On your Mac, choose Apple menu > System Settings, then click Focus in the sidebar. (You may need to scroll down.)
2. Click a Focus on the right.
3. Go to Set a Schedule, click Add Schedule, then do any of the following:
   - *Set up a time-based schedule:* Click Time, enter a start and end time, select the days of the week you want the schedule to operate, then click Done.
     If you want to change a time-based schedule, click it, change the settings, then click Done.
     To temporarily stop using a time-based schedule, click it, turn off Schedule at the top of the window, then click Done.
   - *Set up a location-based schedule:* Click Location, enter a place name in the Search field, select a location, then click Done.
     When you schedule a Focus based on your location, the Focus turns on when you arrive at the location and turns off when you leave.
     To temporarily stop using a location-based schedule, click it, turn off Automation at the top of the window, then click Done.
     You must have Location Services enabled in Privacy settings to use a location.
   - *Set up an app-based schedule:* Click App, enter an app name in the Search field, select an app, then click Done.

When you schedule a Focus based on an app, the Focus turns on when you open the app, and turns off when you close it or switch to another app. To temporarily stop using an app-based schedule, click it, turn off Automation at the top of the window, then click Done.

Customize app behavior

Add a Focus filter to customize how Calendar, Mail, Messages, or Safari behave when a Focus is turned on. For example, choose a set of Tab Groups to appear in Safari while in the Work Focus, or hide your work calendar when you're using the Personal Focus.

1. On your Mac, choose Apple menu > System Settings, then click Focus in the sidebar. (You may need to scroll down.)
2. Click a Focus on the right.
3. Go to Focus Filters, click Add Filter, then do any of the following:
   - *Set up a Focus filter for Calendar:* Click Calendar, select the calendars you want to see when this Focus is on, then click Add.
   - *Set up a Focus filter for Mail:* Click Mail, select the email accounts you want to see when this Focus is on, then click Add.
   - *Set up a Focus filter for Messages:* Click Messages, turn on Filter by People List, then click Add.
   - *Set up a Focus filter for Safari:* Click Safari, click Choose next to Tab Group, select the Tab Group you want to see when this Focus is on, turn "Open external links in your Focus Tab Group" on or off, then click Add.

After you set up a Focus Filter, you can change it or temporarily stop using it. Choose Apple menu > System Settings, click Focus in the sidebar, click a Focus, then click the Focus Filter you want to change. Use the button at the top of the window to turn the Focus Filter on or off, or make changes to the settings. Click Done when you're finished.

To remove a Focus Filter, choose Apple menu > System Settings, click Focus 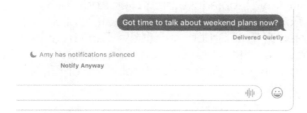 in the sidebar, click a Focus, click the Focus Filter you want to remove, then click Delete App Filter at the bottom of the window.

Keep Focus settings up to date across your Apple devices

When you're signed in with the same Apple ID on all your Apple devices, any changes you make to Focus are reflected on your other devices, and turning a Focus on or off on one device turns it on or off on your other devices.

1. On your Mac, choose Apple menu > System Settings, then click Focus in the sidebar. (You may need to scroll down.)
2. Turn "Share across devices" on or off on the right. (The option is on by default.)

Share your Focus status

You can set an option that lets apps indicate to contacts who send you a message that you've silenced notifications (they don't see which Focus you're using). If something's important, they can choose to notify you anyway.

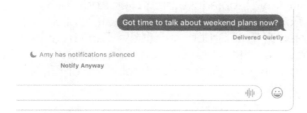

Got time to talk about weekend plans now?

Delivered Quietly

Amy has notifications silenced
Notify Anyway

1. On your Mac, choose Apple menu > System Settings, then click Focus in the sidebar. (You may need to scroll down.)
2. Click "Focus status."
3. Turn on "Share Focus status."

110

4. Below Share From, turn each Focus on or off to specify which ones can share that you have notifications silenced.

Set up Screen Time for yourself

On your Mac, turn on Screen Time to learn how you spend time on your Mac and other devices. When Screen Time is turned on, you can view reports that show app usage, the number of notifications you receive, and how often you use your devices.

1. On your Mac, choose Apple menu > System Settings, then click Screen Time ⏳ in the sidebar. (You may need to scroll down.)
2. If you're a parent/guardian in a Family Sharing group, click the Family Member pop-up menu on the right, then choose yourself.
3. Click App & Website Activity, then click Turn On App & Website Activity.
4. Click the back button ‹, scroll down, then turn on any of the following options:
   - *Share across devices:* Turn on this option if you want Screen Time reports to include time spent on other devices signed in with the same Apple ID. This option is available only when you're signed in with your Apple ID.
   - *Lock Screen Time Settings:* Turn on this option to require a passcode to access Screen Time settings and allow additional time when limits expire. *Note:* If the family member has an administrator account, you're prompted to convert it to a standard account.
5. You can also do any of the following in Screen Time settings:
   - Click App & Website Activity, Notifications, or Pickups, then view your app and device usage.
   - Click Downtime, then set up a downtime schedule.
   - Click App Limits, then set time limits for apps and websites.
   - Click Always Allowed, then choose apps that can be used at any time.

- Click Screen Distance, then receive alerts when you're holding a device too close.
- Click Communication Limits, then set communication limits.
- Click Communication Safety, then choose to check for sensitive photos.
- Click Content & Privacy, then set up content & privacy restrictions.

Use Dictation

With Dictation, you can enter text just by speaking, anywhere that you can type it.

On a Mac with Apple silicon, Dictation requests are processed on your device for supported languages—no internet connection is required. When you dictate in a search box, dictated text may be sent to the search provider in order to process the search. Additionally, you can dictate text of any length without a timeout. You can turn off Dictation manually, or it stops automatically when no speech is detected for 30 seconds.

When you dictate on an Intel-based Mac or in a language that doesn't support on-device dictation, your dictated utterances are sent to Apple to process your requests.

Note: Dictation may not be available in all languages or in all countries or regions, and features may vary. To learn more about how Apple protects your information and lets you choose what you share, click About Ask Siri, Dictation & Privacy at the bottom of Keyboard settings.

If you need to dictate text and control your Mac using your voice instead of a keyboard and trackpad, use Voice Control.

Turn on Dictation

1. On your Mac, choose Apple menu > System Settings, then click Keyboard ⌨ in the sidebar. (You may need to scroll down.)
2. Go to Dictation on the right, then turn it on. If a prompt appears, click Enable.
3. If you're asked if you want to improve Siri and Dictation, do one of the following:
    - *Share audio recordings:* Click Share Audio Recordings to allow Apple to store audio of your Siri and Dictation interactions from your Mac. Apple may review a sample of stored audio.
    - *Don't share audio recordings:* Click Not Now.
4. If you change your mind later and want to share or stop sharing audio recordings, choose Apple menu > System Settings, then click Privacy & Security ✋ in the sidebar. (You may need to scroll down.) Go to Analytics & Improvements on the right, then turn on or off the Improve Siri & Dictation option.
Note: You can delete the audio interactions (which are associated with a random identifier and less than six months old) whenever you like.

5. To dictate using another language, click the Edit button next to Languages, then select a language and dialect. (To remove a language, deselect it.)

To learn more about how Apple protects your information and lets you choose what you share, click About Ask Siri, Dictation & Privacy at the bottom of Keyboard settings.

Dictate text

1. In an app on your Mac, place the insertion point where you want the dictated text to appear.
2. Press 🎙️ if available in the row of function keys, use the Dictation keyboard shortcut, or choose Edit > Start Dictation.

   Note: Press and release 🎙️ to start Dictation; press and hold 🎙️ to activate Siri (Siri must be enabled).
3. When a microphone icon 🎙️ appears above or below a highlighted cursor, or you hear the tone that signals your Mac is ready for dictation, dictate your text.
   On a Mac with Apple silicon, you can type text even while dictating; there's no need to stop dictation. The microphone icon disappears while you type, and then reappears after you stop typing, so you can continue dictating.
4. To insert an emoji or a punctuation mark, or perform simple formatting tasks, do any of the following:
   - Say the name of an emoji, like "heart emoji" or "car emoji."
   - Say the name of the punctuation mark, such as "exclamation mark."
   - Say "new line" (equivalent to pressing the Return key once) or "new paragraph" (equivalent to pressing the Return key twice). The new line or new paragraph appear when you're done dictating.
     Note: In supported languages, Dictation automatically inserts commas, periods, and question marks for you as you dictate. To turn this feature off, choose Apple menu > System Settings, then click Keyboard in the sidebar. (You may need to scroll down.) Go to Dictation on the right, then turn off Auto-punctuation.

5. If you set up Dictation for multiple languages and want to switch languages as you dictate, click the language next to the microphone or click ⊕, then choose the language you want to use.
6. When you're done, press the Dictation keyboard shortcut or the Escape key. Dictation stops automatically when no speech is detected for 30 seconds.

Ambiguous text is underlined in blue. For example, you may get the result "flour" when you intended the word "flower." If this is the case, click the underlined word and select an alternative. You can also type or dictate the correct text.

Set the Dictation keyboard shortcut

You can choose a specific Dictation keyboard shortcut or create one of your own.

Tip: If 🎤 is available in the row of function keys, you can press it to start Dictation or use the keyboard shortcut.

1. On your Mac, choose Apple menu > System Settings, then click Keyboard ⌨ in the sidebar. (You may need to scroll down.)
2. Go to Dictation on the right, click the pop-up menu next to Shortcut, then choose a shortcut to start Dictation.
   To create a shortcut that's not in the list, choose Customize, then press the keys you want to use. For example, you could press Option-Z.

Note: When you choose a Dictation keyboard shortcut, depending on your Mac model, the "Press fn key to" or "Press ⊕ key to" option in Keyboard settings may change automatically. For example, if you choose Press Fn (Function) Key Twice as the Dictation Shortcut option, the Keyboard settings option changes to Start Dictation (Press Fn Twice) automatically.

For more help with Keyboard options, click the Help button ⑦ in Keyboard settings.

Change the microphone used for Dictation

The microphone source in Keyboard settings shows which device your Mac is currently using to listen for Dictation.

1. On your Mac, choose Apple menu > System Settings, then click Keyboard ⌨ in the sidebar. (You may need to scroll down.)
2. Go to Dictation on the right, click the pop-up menu next to "Microphone source," then choose the microphone you want to use for Dictation.
   If you choose Automatic, your Mac listens to the device you're most likely to use for Dictation.

Turn off Dictation

1. On your Mac, choose Apple menu > System Settings, then click Keyboard ⌨ in the sidebar. (You may need to scroll down.)
2. Go to Dictation on the right, then turn it off.

Send emails

You can send email, save emails as drafts, and schedule emails to send later.

Before you can send an email, you need to add at least one email account in the Mail app.

Send an email

1. In the Mail app ✉ on your Mac, click the New Message button ☑ in the Mail toolbar.
2. In the To field, type the email address you want to send the email to.
   You can also send emails to a group of email addresses

from your Contacts app, or hide everyone's email address to protect the privacy of your recipients.

3. Enter the subject of your email in the Subject field.
4. In the Message field (below the subject), type your message. You can format the text of your email and send photos and other files as attachments to your email.
5. Click the Send button ⬦ .

Save a draft

1. In the Mail app ✉ on your Mac, make sure you're in the message that you want to save.
2. Choose File > Save.
   You can also close the message window, then click Save in the dialog that appears.

When you want to return to your draft, you can find it in the Drafts mailbox (from the Favorites bar or the Mail sidebar).

Schedule an email

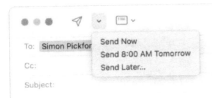

In the Mail app ✉ on your Mac, do one of the following:

- *Schedule an email:* Click the pop-up menu next to the Send button ⬦ , then choose a time, or choose Send Later to set a date and time.
  The email appears in the Send Later mailbox in the Mail sidebar.
- *Change the scheduled time for an email:* Double-click the email in the Send Later mailbox, then click Edit in the top-right corner.
- *Prevent a scheduled email from sending:* Select the email in the Send Later mailbox, then click the Delete button 🗑 .

117

Send text messages

Messages on Mac don't have to be boring. After you set up your Mac, you can send messages to one person, a group of people, or a business and include text, photos, animated effects, and more. You can express yourself in all sorts of ways:

- Tapbacks
- Photos and videos
- Photos, scans, and sketches (from an iPhone or iPad)
- Stickers and images
- Audio messages
- Message effects

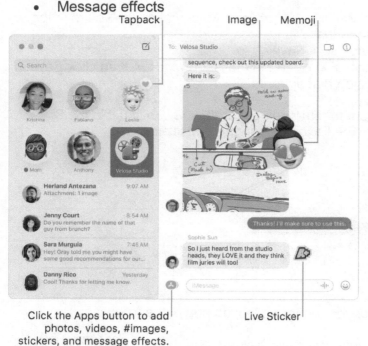

Tapback | Image | Memoji

Click the Apps button to add photos, videos, #images, stickers, and message effects.

Live Sticker

1. In the Messages app 💬 on your Mac, click the Compose button 📝 to start a new message (or use the Touch Bar).
2. In the To field, type the name, email address, or phone number of the person you want to send a message to. As you type, Messages suggests matching addresses from your Contacts app 📇 or from people you've previously sent messages to.

   You can also click the Add button ⊕ to the right of the To

118

field. Click a contact in the list, then click the email address or phone number.
Note: If you're restricted to sending and receiving messages with only certain people, an hourglass icon ⌛ appears next to those people you can't send messages to.

3. Enter your message in the field at the bottom of the window. You can use typing suggestions, if available.

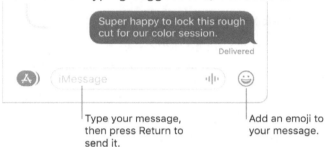

Type your message, then press Return to send it.

Add an emoji to your message.

Siri: Say something like: "Message Mom that I'll be late."

4. Press Return on your keyboard or click the Send button 🔼 to send the message.

Make a FaceTime video call

With FaceTime video calls, people can see and talk to each other, using an Apple device that meets these requirements. FaceTime video calls use your Mac's Wi-Fi connection.

Make a FaceTime video call

1. In the FaceTime app 🎥 on your Mac, click New FaceTime.
2. In the New FaceTime window, enter the email address or phone number of the person you want to call. You may need to press Return.
   Tip: If the person is in your Contacts, you can just enter their name, or select them from Suggested. You can also add contacts from the New FaceTime window.
3. Click FaceTime, or use the Touch Bar.

Siri: Say something like: "FaceTime mom."

Answer a FaceTime video call

When you're signed in and FaceTime is turned on, you can accept calls, even if FaceTime isn't open.

On your Mac, do one of the following when a notification appears in the top-right corner of the screen:

- *Accept an incoming call:* Click Accept.

- *Accept a video call as an audio call:* Click ∨ next to Accept, then choose Answer as Audio. When you're in an audio call or a phone call, the camera is automatically off.
- *Accept a call and end the current call:* Click End & Accept.
- *Decline a call:* Click Decline.

  You can also click ∨ next to Decline to send a text message or create a reminder.
  Tip: If the call came from someone you don't want to receive calls from, you can block the caller.

After you're on a call, you can add more people or share a link to it.

Decline a FaceTime video call

When you're signed in and FaceTime is turned on, you can decline calls, even if FaceTime isn't open.

On your Mac, do one of the following when a notification appears in the top-right corner of the screen:

- *Decline a call:* Click Decline.
  The caller sees that you're not available for a call.
  Tip: If the call came from someone you don't want to receive calls from, you can block the caller.
- *Decline a call and send a message using iMessage:* Click ∨ next to Decline, choose Reply with Message, type your message, then click Send. Both you and the caller must be signed in to iMessage.

- *Decline a call and set a reminder to call back later:* Click ∨ next to Decline, then choose how long you want to wait to receive a reminder. When the time comes, you receive a

notification—click it to view the reminder, then click the link
in the reminder to start the call.

End a FaceTime video call

To end the call, move the pointer over the call window, then click the
Leave Call button ⊗ (or use the Touch Bar).

Edit photos and videos

With the Photos editing tools, you can quickly crop and rotate
photos, apply filters, enhance photos, and more. You can duplicate
photos to try out adjustments, and copy adjustments to other
photos. If you don't like the changes you made to a photo, you can
undo them.

Edit a photo or video

1. In the Photos app 🌸 on your Mac, do one of the following:
   ○ Double-click a photo or video thumbnail, then click
     Edit in the toolbar.
   ○ Select a photo or video thumbnail, then press Return.
2. Do any of the following:

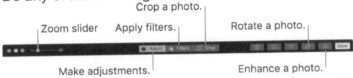

Crop a photo.
Zoom slider   Apply filters.   Rotate a photo.
Make adjustments.   Enhance a photo.

   ○ *Zoom in or out on a photo:* Click or drag the Zoom
     slider.
   ○ *Make adjustments:* Click Adjust to display the
     adjustment tools.
   ○ *Apply filters:* Click Filters to display filters you can
     apply to change the look of your photo or video.
   ○ *Crop the image:* Click Crop to display the options for
     cropping a photo or video.
   ○ *Rotate a photo or video:* Click the Rotate button ⟲
     in the toolbar to rotate the image counterclockwise.
     Continue clicking until you get the orientation you

121

want. Option-click the button to rotate the image clockwise.

- ○ *Automatically enhance a photo or video:* Click the Auto Enhance button ✦✧ to have the color and contrast of your photo or video adjusted automatically. To remove the changes, press Command-Z or click Revert to Original.

3. To stop editing, click Done or press Return.

While you're editing a photo or video, you can press the arrow keys to switch to other items.

Duplicate a photo

To create different versions of a photo or video, you duplicate it and work on the copy.

1. In the Photos app 🌸 on your Mac, select the item you want to copy.
2. Choose Image > Duplicate 1 Photo (or press Command-D). If you're duplicating a Live Photo, click Duplicate to include the video portion, or Duplicate as Still Photo to include just the still image.

Compare photos or videos before and after editing

While editing an item, you can compare the edited version with the original.

1. In the Photos app 🌸 on your Mac, double-click a photo or video to open it, then click Edit in the toolbar.
2. To see the original image, click and hold the Without Adjustments button, or press and hold the M key. Release the button or the M key to see the item with edits.

Click and hold to see your photo without adjustments.

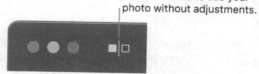

Copy and paste edits

After you edit a photo or video, you can copy the edits that you've made and paste them on other items. You can paste edits onto multiple items at a time.

Note: You can't copy and paste the settings from the retouch tool, red-eye tool, crop tool, or third-party extensions.

1. In the Photos app on your Mac, double-click an item you've made adjustments to, then click Edit in the toolbar.
2. Choose Image > Copy Edits.
3. Click the item (or Command-click multiple items) to which you want to apply the adjustments.
4. Choose Image > Paste Edits.

You can also Control-click an item in editing view and choose Copy Edits or Paste Edits.

Undo your changes

You can quickly remove changes to a photo or video.

In the Photos app on your Mac, do any of the following:

- *Undo the last change you made:* Choose Edit > Undo, or press Command-Z.
- *Undo all your changes and restore the original image:* Select the photo or video, then choose Image > Revert to Original.

Use Live Text to interact with text in a photo

In Photos, you can use Live Text to copy and use the text that appears in a photo. For example, you can copy the text of a roadside sign and paste it into a text message or email.

1. In the Photos app  on your Mac, open a photo that shows text.
2. Position the pointer over the text, then drag to select it.
3. Do any of the following:
   - *Copy text:* Control-click your selection and choose Copy (or press Command-C). You can then paste the text into another document or app.
   - *Look up the meaning of text:* Control-click your selection and choose Look Up [*text*].
   - *Translate text:* Control-click your selection, choose Translate [*text*], then choose a language.
     Note: Translation isn't available in all languages and may not be available in some countries or regions.
   - *Search the web for the text:* Control-click your selection and choose Search with [*web search engine*].
   - *Share the text with others:* Control-click your selection, choose Share, then choose how you want to share the text.
   - *Contact a phone number:* Control-click your selection or click the down arrow ⌄, then choose to call the number, start a FaceTime video or audio call, or send a message to the number.

- ○ *Contact an email address:* Control-click your selection or click the down arrow ∨ , then choose to compose an email or add the email address to Contacts.
- ○ *Go to a website:* Control-click your selection or click the down arrow ∨ , then open the link in your browser or use Quick Look to view the website information.

Start a Quick Note

With Quick Note, you can jot down ideas and add links, no matter what you're doing on your Mac. Your Quick Note stays visible on the screen while it's open, so you can easily select and add information from other apps.

Start a Quick Note

If you're working in another app and want to write something down, you can easily start a Quick Note. Do one of the following:

- *Use the keyboard shortcut:* Press and hold the Fn key or Globe key ⊕ , then press Q.
- *Use hot corners:* Move the pointer to the bottom-right corner of the screen (the default hot corner for Quick Note), then click the note that appears. T
- *Use Safari.*

To close a Quick Note, click the red Close button ✕ in the top left corner of the note. To open the Quick Note again, use any of the methods above.

To always start a new Quick Note (instead of opening the previous one), choose Notes > Settings, then deselect "Always resume to last Quick Note."

Add Safari links to a Quick Note

125

1. In the Safari app ⊘ on your Mac, open the webpage you want to link to.
2. Click the Share button ⬆, then choose New Quick Note or Add to Quick Note.
   When you return to the linked content in the webpage, a thumbnail of the Quick Note appears in the corner of the screen to remind you of what you noted earlier.

You can also add links to webpages and other apps in Notes.

Add content from Safari to a Quick Note

You can highlight text in a webpage and add it directly to a Quick Note.

1. In the Safari app ⊘ on your Mac, open a webpage, then select the text you want to add to a Quick Note.
2. Control-click the text, then choose New Quick Note or Add to Quick Note.
   A link appears in the Quick Note, and the text in Safari is highlighted. When you visit the webpage again later, the text is still highlighted.

To remove the highlights, delete the Safari link from the Quick Note.

Edit a Quick Note

Your Quick Notes appear in the Quick Notes folder in the Notes app. You can edit them to add tables, tags, and more.

Note: You can't lock a Quick Note.

Get directions

You can get directions for driving, walking, taking public transportation, or cycling. When driving, you can add multiple stops to your route. You can also send the directions to your iPhone, iPad, or Apple Watch for quick access on the go.

Note: Directions for multiple stops are not available in all countries or regions.

Click to see directions for an alternate route.

Drag to reorder the locations.

Click a step to zoom in on it.

Get directions

1. In the Maps app on your Mac, do one of the following:
   - Click the Directions button ⟳ in the toolbar, then enter your starting location and destination.
   - Click your destination, such as a landmark or pin on a map, then click Directions in the place card. If your current location is showing, Maps uses it as your starting location, but you can enter a different one. You can also drag the Reorder button ☰ next to a location to swap your starting and ending locations.
2. **Tip:** You can also search for the name of someone in your contacts, or someone who shares their location with you in Find My (not available in all countries or regions), and get directions to their address or location.

3. Click the Drive 🚗, Walk 🚶, Transit 🚆, or Cycle 🚲 button.
4. Click the Trip Details button ❯ next to a route to see the directions list.
   If you're driving, directions can include:
   - *Electric vehicle routing:* See charging stations along your route and keep track of your current charge (if you have a compatible vehicle).
   - *Congestion zones:* For major cities like London, Paris, and Singapore, congestion zones help reduce traffic in dense areas. You can get a route around these zones during hours when they are in force.
   - *License plate restrictions:* For Chinese cities that limit access to dense areas, you can get a route through or around a restricted area based on your eligibility.
5. If you're cycling, directions are available in select cities.
6. Do any of the following:
   - *Zoom in on a step:* Click the step in the directions list.
   - *Choose when to leave or arrive:* For driving and public transportation, click Plan to choose when you intend to leave or want to arrive.
   - *Close the directions list:* Click the Trip Details button ⌄ again.

Get directions to multiple stops when driving

1. In the Maps app 🗺 on your Mac, do one of the following:
   - Click the Directions button ↱ in the toolbar, then enter your starting location and first stop.
   - Click your first stop, such as a landmark or pin on a map, then click Directions in the place card.
     If your current location is showing, Maps uses it as your starting location, but you can enter a different one.
2. Click the Drive button 🚗.
3. Click Add stop, then click a recently searched location, or search for a location and click the result in the list.
   Repeat to add additional stops.
4. Do any of the following:

- Change the order of stops: Drag the Reorder button ≡ next to a stop to move it up or down the list.
- Change a stop: Click the stop, then click a suggested similar location, or search for a location and click the result in the list.
- Delete a stop: Move the pointer over a stop, then click the Remove button ⊗.

Automatically get directions on your iPhone or iPad

After you search a route on Mac, you can easily open it in the Maps app on your iPhone (with iOS 16 or later) or iPad (with iPadOS 16 or later) where you've signed in with the same Apple ID.

1. Open the Maps app on iPhone or iPad.
2. Scroll down in the search card to Recents, then tap the route.

Send directions to your iPhone, iPad, or Apple Watch

You can send directions or a location to your other devices. (You must be signed in using the same Apple ID on both your device and your Mac.)

Note: You can only share driving routes that don't contain multiple stops.

1. In the Maps app 🗺 on your Mac, click a location on the map, click Directions, then make any adjustments you want.
2. Click the Share button ⬆ in the toolbar, then choose the device you want to send directions to.
3. Open the Maps app on your device to view the directions.

Use Apple devices together

Work across devices using Continuity

With Continuity, you can use your Mac together with your other Apple devices to work smarter and move seamlessly between your devices.

To use Continuity features, sign in with the same Apple ID on all your devices. In addition, your devices must have Wi-Fi and Bluetooth® turned on, and meet system requirements.

AirDrop

AirDrop lets you quickly share photos, videos, contacts, and anything else, with anyone near you—wirelessly. It makes sharing to iPhone, iPad, iPod touch, and Mac as simple as dragging and dropping.

AirPlay to Mac

Share, play, or present content from another Apple device to the screen of your Mac.

Auto Unlock and Approve with Apple Watch

Use your Apple Watch to unlock your Mac or approve authentication requests from your Mac, without having to enter a password.

Continuity Camera

Use your iPhone as a webcam on Mac, or take a picture or scan a document with your nearby iPhone or iPad and have it appear instantly on your Mac.

Continuity Markup

Edit a PDF document or image on your Mac and display it on your nearby iPhone or iPad, where you can write and sketch on it using

Markup tools—and Apple Pencil on iPad—and instantly view the changes on your Mac.

Continuity Sketch

Draw a sketch using your nearby iPhone or iPad and have the sketch appear instantly on your Mac.

Handoff

Start a document, an email, or a message on one device and pick up where you left off on another device. Handoff works with apps like Mail, Safari, Maps, Messages, Reminders, Calendar, Contacts, Pages, Numbers, and Keynote.

Instant Hotspot

No Wi-Fi? No problem. Your Mac can connect to the internet using the personal hotspot on your iPhone or iPad when they're within range of each other—no setup is required. Your iPhone or iPad automatically appears in the Wi-Fi menu on your Mac—just select it to turn on your hotspot.

Phone Calls

When you want to make or answer a phone call, don't reach for your iPhone—use your Mac. You can start calls from FaceTime, Contacts, Safari, Mail, Maps, Spotlight, and many other apps. When someone calls you, a notification appears. Just click the notification to answer.

Sidecar

When you use your iPad as a second display, you can have your iPad show the same apps and windows as your Mac, or extend your workspace by showing different apps and windows.

SMS Messages

Send and receive SMS and MMS text messages right from your Mac. When friends send you text messages, regardless of what phone they have, you can respond from whichever device is closest. All the messages that appear on your iPhone appear on your Mac, too.

Universal Clipboard

Copy text, images, photos, and videos on one Apple device and then paste the content on another Apple device. For example, you can copy a recipe from Safari on your Mac, then paste it into Notes on your nearby iPhone.

Universal Control

When your Mac is near another Mac or iPad, you can use a single keyboard and trackpad, or a connected mouse, to work across the devices. You can even drag content between them—for example, you can sketch a drawing with Apple Pencil on iPad, then drag it to your Mac to drop into a Keynote presentation.

Use iPhone as a webcam

With Continuity Camera, you can use your iPhone as your Mac webcam or microphone, and take advantage of the powerful iPhone camera and additional video effects. You can connect wirelessly, or with a USB cable for a wired connection.

Before you begin

Before you can use the Continuity Camera feature, you need to do the following:

- Make sure your Mac has macOS 13 or later and your iPhone has iOS 16 or later.
  Note: To enable all Continuity Camera options, your Mac must have macOS 14 and your iPhone must have iOS 17.
- Sign in to both devices with the same Apple ID.
- Turn on Wi-Fi and Bluetooth® on both devices.
- Make sure your devices meet system requirements.
- Mount your iPhone.

Use your iPhone as a webcam or microphone

1. On your Mac, open any app that has access to the camera or microphone, like FaceTime or Photo Booth.
2. In the app's menu bar or settings, choose your iPhone as the camera or microphone.
   The Continuity app opens on your iPhone and begins streaming audio or video from the rear camera to your Mac. *Note:* In order to use your iPhone as a microphone on a Mac without a built-in camera, the iPhone must be in landscape orientation and stationary, and have its screen turned off. Alternatively, you can plug your iPhone into your Mac with a USB cable.
3. Do any of the following:
   - *Pause the video or audio:* On your iPhone, tap Pause, or swipe up to unlock it.
   - *Resume the video or audio:* On your iPhone, tap Resume, or press the side button or Sleep/Wake button to lock it.
   - *Stop using your iPhone as a webcam or microphone:* On your Mac, quit the app.
   - *Remove your iPhone as an option:* On your iPhone, tap Disconnect, then confirm that you would like to disconnect. Your iPhone is removed from the camera and microphone lists in apps, and also from the list of sound input devices in Sound settings.
     To add your iPhone back, connect it to your Mac with a USB cable.

If you need to charge your iPhone while Continuity Camera is turned on, use a USB cable for best results.

Automatically switch to the iPhone camera

Your Mac can automatically switch to using iPhone as a camera input for certain Mac apps, like FaceTime and Photo Booth. To do this, your iPhone must:

- Be close to your Mac
- Have its screen off
- Be in landscape orientation

- Have its rear camera or cameras facing you and be unobstructed
- Not be in a pocket or lying flat on a desk
- Be stationary

If you've used your iPhone as a webcam on your Mac before, other Mac apps may also remember it as the preferred camera.

Make your iPhone the default microphone

You can make your iPhone the default microphone for your Mac.

1. On your Mac, choose Apple menu > System Settings, then click Sound in the sidebar. (You may need to scroll down.)
2. Select your iPhone in the list of sound input devices. The Continuity app opens on your iPhone and starts capturing audio.

Turn on Desk View and video effects

When you use your iPhone as a Mac webcam, you can use the Video icon in the menu bar to use video conferencing features. For example, Desk View shows a top-down view of your desk, and Studio Light dims the background and illuminates your face.

If you don't see your iPhone as a camera or microphone option

If you don't see your iPhone in the camera or microphone list in an app or Sound settings, try the following.

1. Connect it to your Mac with a USB cable and check again. (If it's already connected with a cable, disconnect it and reconnect it.)
2. Check the following:
   - Your iPhone is an iPhone XR or later.
   - Your iPhone has iOS 16 or later.

- Your Mac has macOS 13 or later.
- Your iPhone has Continuity Camera turned on in Settings > General > AirPlay & Handoff.
- Your iPhone recognizes the Mac as a trusted computer.
- Your iPhone and Mac have Wi-Fi, Bluetooth, and two-factor authentication turned on.
- Your iPhone and Mac are signed in with the same Apple ID. (This feature doesn't work with Managed Apple IDs.)
- Your iPhone and Mac are within 30 feet of each other.
- Your iPhone isn't sharing its cellular connection, and your Mac isn't sharing its internet connection.
- Your chosen video app is updated to the latest version.

Note: If your Mac doesn't have a built-in camera, your iPhone can be seen as a camera as long as it meets all of the conditions to automatically switch to the iPhone camera. You can also plug your iPhone into your Mac with a USB cable.

You can also use Continuity Camera to scan documents or take a picture of something nearby and have it appear instantly on your Mac.

Use iPhone with Desk View

When using your iPhone as a webcam, you can use Desk View with FaceTime and other apps to show your face and an overhead view of your desk at the same time, with no complicated setup.

Note: Desk View is only available with iPhone 11 or later, excluding iPhone SE.

Use Desk View with FaceTime

1. On your Mac, open the FaceTime app .
2. Attach your iPhone to your Mac with a stand accessory, then use your iPhone as a webcam.

3. Start your video call, then click the Desk View button in the top-right corner of the video window.
Desk View opens, which mimics an overhead camera and shows a top-down view of your desk.
4. Use the Desk View setup window to align your desk with the camera. To zoom in or out, drag the onscreen control at the bottom of the window. When you're ready to share your desk view on the video call, click Share Desk View.
5. To turn off Desk View, click the Screen Share button

in the top left of the Desk View window, then choose Close Window (or choose Desk View > Quit Desk View in the menu bar).

Use Desk View with other apps

1. On your Mac, open an app that captures video.
2. Attach your iPhone to your Mac with a stand accessory, then use your iPhone as a webcam.
3. Click the Video icon in the menu bar, then click Desk View.
Desk View opens, which mimics an overhead camera and shows a top-down view of your desk.
Tip: You can also open Desk View by searching for it in Spotlight.
4. Use the Desk View setup window to align your desk with the camera. To zoom in or out, drag the onscreen control at the bottom of the window. When you're ready, click Start Desk View.
5. To share what's on your desk in a third-party app, use the app's screen sharing feature to select the Desk View window for sharing. To find out how, see the developer's instructions or explore the app's menus and settings.
6. To turn off Desk View, close the Desk View window or choose Desk View > Quit Desk View in the menu bar.

Stream audio and video with AirPlay

AirPlay lets you use a Wi-Fi connection to wirelessly stream music, videos, photos, and more from your Mac to your favorite speakers (such as HomePod mini), your Apple TV, and certain smart TVs.

Just make sure your Mac and other devices are on the same Wi-Fi network.

Listen to music on your favorite speakers

Get that big band sound by streaming music from your Mac to a HomePod—or two—or any other AirPlay 2-enabled speaker. On your Mac, open the Apple Music app 🎵, queue your tunes, click 🔘 in the playback controls, then select a speaker.

Tip: Broaden your horizons during dinner by listening to your favorite travel podcast.

Play movies and more on the big screen

It's easy to play movies, TV shows, and videos on the big screen of your TV. On your Mac, open the Apple TV app 📺, start the show, click 🔲 in the playback controls, then select your Apple TV or smart TV.

Tip: Found a great video on the web you want to watch with your friends? Use AirPlay right in the Safari app.

Share photos with everyone in the room

With AirPlay mirroring and your Apple TV, everyone in the room can view what's playing on your Mac—like a slideshow of wedding photos in the Photos app—on your big screen TV. On your Mac, click Control Center  in the menu bar, click Screen Mirroring, then select your Apple TV or smart TV.

If your Mac and other Apple devices support AirPlay to Mac, you can listen to audio and play video from another device on your Mac.

Use one keyboard and mouse to control Mac and iPad

With Universal Control, you can work across up to three devices (for example, a Mac and an iPad) using a single keyboard and mouse or trackpad. You can also drag items between devices.

To use Universal Control, make sure of the following:

- You're using supported models of Mac and iPad.
- Your Mac has macOS 12.3 or later, and your iPad has iPadOS 15.4 or later.
- You're signed in with the same Apple ID with two-factor authentication on all your devices.
- You have Wi-Fi, Bluetooth®, and Handoff turned on in System Settings (on your Mac) and in Settings (on your iPad).

Connect your Mac to another Mac or iPad to use Universal Control

With Universal Control, you can establish a connection between your Mac and a nearby device, and then use a single keyboard and mouse or trackpad to work across the devices.

Note: If you don't use Universal Control for a period of time, you may need to establish the connection again.

Do one of the following:

- On your Mac, use your mouse or trackpad to move the pointer to the right or left edge of the Mac screen. When a border appears at the edge of the Mac screen, move the pointer past the border, until the pointer appears on the other device.

- On your Mac, choose Apple menu > System Settings, then click Displays in the sidebar. (You may need to scroll down.) Click the pop-up menu on the right, then choose a device below Link Keyboard and Mouse. Use your mouse or trackpad to move the pointer past the edge of the Mac screen until it appears on the other device.

- On your Mac, click Control Center in the menu bar, click Display, then choose a device below "Link keyboard and mouse to." Use your mouse or trackpad to move the pointer past the edge of the Mac screen until it appears on the other device.

The direction in which you move the pointer when establishing the connection determines which side of the display you use to connect your devices. You can adjust this behavior by changing the arrangement of the devices in Displays settings. Click the image of the display, then drag it to the desired position.

You can set your Mac to automatically reconnect to any nearby Mac or iPad. Choose Apple menu > System Settings, then click Displays in the sidebar. (You may need to scroll down.) Click Advanced on the right, then select "Automatically reconnect to any nearby Mac or iPad."

Disconnect your Mac from another device

After you establish a connection between devices using Universal Control, the connection remains until either of the devices goes to sleep or you disconnect them.

1. On your Mac, choose Apple menu > System Settings, then click Displays 🔆 in the sidebar. (You may need to scroll down.)
2. Select your display on the right, then click Disconnect.

Turn off Universal Control

You can turn off Universal Control to prevent your Mac from connecting to other devices to use a keyboard and mouse or trackpad.

1. On your Mac, choose Apple menu > System Settings, then click Displays 🔆 in the sidebar. (You may need to scroll down.)
2. Click Advanced on the right, then do one of the following:
   - *Turn off all Universal Control connections:* Turn off "Allow your pointer and keyboard to move between any nearby Mac or iPad."
   - *Prevent a connection when moving the pointer to the edge of the screen:* Turn off "Push through the edge of a display to connect to a nearby Mac or iPad."

You can set an option to temporarily disable Universal Control whenever you zoom in on the screen of your Mac, so that it's easier to zoom in along the edge of the screen.

Hand off between devices

With Handoff, you can start something on one Apple device (Mac, iPhone, iPad, or Apple Watch) and then seamlessly pick it up on another device. For example, start answering an email on your iPhone, then finish it in Mail on your Mac. You can use Handoff with many Apple apps—for example, Calendar, Contacts, Pages, and Safari. Some third-party apps may also work with Handoff.

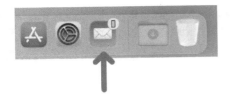

To use Handoff, your Apple devices must meet Continuity system requirements. They must also have Wi-Fi, Bluetooth®, and Handoff turned on in System Settings (on your Mac) and in Settings (on your iOS and iPadOS devices). You must be signed in with the same Apple ID on all your devices.

Tip: When Handoff is on, you can use Universal Clipboard to copy and paste text, images, photos, and videos across devices. You can also copy files between Mac computers.

Turn Handoff on or off

Note: If a Handoff option isn't available on your device, it doesn't work with Handoff.

- *On your Mac:* Choose Apple menu > System Settings, click General in the sidebar, click AirDrop & Handoff on the right, then turn "Allow Handoff between this Mac and your iCloud devices" on or off. (You may need to scroll down.)
- *On iPad, iPhone, or iPod touch:* Go to Settings > General > AirPlay & Handoff, then turn Handoff on or off.
- *On Apple Watch:* Open the Apple Watch app on iPhone, go to My Watch > General, then turn Enable Handoff on or off.

Hand off between devices

- *From your Mac to an iOS or iPadOS device:* The Handoff icon of the app you're using on your Mac appears on your iPhone (at the bottom of the app switcher) or your iPad or iPod touch (at the end of the Dock). Tap to continue working in the app.
- *From an iOS or iPadOS device or Apple Watch to your Mac:* The Handoff icon of the app you're using on your iPhone, iPad, iPod touch, or Apple Watch appears on your Mac near

141

the right end of the Dock (or the bottom, depending on the Dock position). Click the icon to continue working in the app. You can also press Command-Tab to quickly switch to the app that has the Handoff icon.

Unlock your Mac with Apple Watch

When you're wearing your Apple Watch and are near your Mac, you can use your Apple Watch to unlock your Mac or approve app requests, without having to enter a password.

Note: To use these features, make sure you're wearing your unlocked Apple Watch with your Mac nearby, you're signed in with the same Apple ID on your Mac (a mid-2013 or later model) and Apple Watch, and two-factor authentication is turned on for your Apple ID.

Turn on Auto Unlock and Approve with Apple Watch

1. Choose Apple menu > System Settings, then click Touch ID & Password in the sidebar. (You may need to scroll down.)
2. Go to Apple Watch on the right, then turn on the option next to the name of your watch.
   This option is only available if your Apple Watch has watchOS 6 or later installed.

Unlock your Mac

Wake your Mac from its idle state by pressing any keyboard key or, on a Mac laptop, by opening the display. The screen indicates that your Mac is being unlocked.

Approve app requests

When an app requires authentication on your Mac—for example, to view passwords, unlock notes or settings, and approve app installations—an approval request from your Mac appears on your Apple Watch.

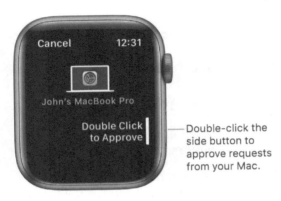

Double-click the
side button to
approve requests
from your Mac.

Double-click the side button of your Apple Watch to approve the task request.

If you're not sure if your Mac supports Auto Unlock and Approve with Apple Watch, choose Apple menu > About This Mac, click More Info, then click System Report at the bottom of the window. In the sidebar, in the Network section, click Wi-Fi, then look on the right for "Auto Unlock: Supported."

If you're the administrator for another user on your Mac, you can log in to their user account and turn on Auto Unlock or Approve with Apple Watch for them, as long as their Apple ID uses two-factor authentication and their Apple Watch has the required version of watchOS installed.

Make and receive phone calls on your Mac

When you want to make or receive a phone call, you don't have to reach for your iPhone—you can use your Mac. When someone calls you, a notification appears on your Mac and you can take the call—and even use Real-Time Text (RTT) for your phone calls, if your carrier supports it.

Note: Phone calls you make and receive on your Mac use cellular minutes—cellular charges may apply.

Make phone calls from apps on your Mac

1. In the FaceTime app ▣ on your Mac, sign in and make sure FaceTime is turned on.
2. Set up your iPhone and Mac for phone calls, if you haven't done so already.
3. Depending on the macOS app you want to use for your phone call, do one of the following:
    o *FaceTime:* Click New FaceTime, enter a phone number in the pop-up window, press Return, then click ⌄ to choose the phone number to call.
    If you have a card for the person in the Contacts app, you can just enter the person's name, or select them from Suggested.
    If you set up RTT phone calls, you can choose to make an RTT call.
    Note: You can also invite a person to a call by sending them an SMS message.
    o *Contacts:* Select a contact, move the pointer over a phone number, then click the Phone button 📞.
    If you set up RTT phone calls, you can choose to make an RTT call.
    o *Safari:* Click a phone number on a webpage, then click Call.
    o *Mail:* Place the pointer over a phone number in an email, click the pop-up menu ⌄, then choose how you want to make the call.
    o *Maps:* Click a place of interest, then click the Call button 📞.
    o *Spotlight:* Enter the name of a person or place in the Spotlight search field, then click a search suggestion to view in Spotlight. Move the pointer over a phone number, then click the Phone button 📞.
    o *Calendar:* Open an event, look for an underlined blue phone number in the event details, click the number, then click Call. Or, for a FaceTime video call added to a calendar event, click Join.
    o *Reminders:* Open the reminders list, click an underlined blue phone number, then click Call.

    ◦ *Find My:* Open the People list, then select a name. Click the Info button ⓘ, click Contact, then click the Call button 📞.

Note: If you're restricted to calls with only certain people, an hourglass icon ⏳ appears next to those people you can't call.

Answer phone calls on your Mac

On your Mac, when a notification appears in the top-right corner of the screen, do one of the following in the notification:

- *Accept an incoming call:* Click Accept.
  If the person calling you has set up RTT for the call and you want to answer it that way, click RTT.
- *Decline a call:* Click Decline.
  Tip: If the call came from someone you don't want to receive calls from, you can block the caller.
- *Decline a call and send a message using iMessage:* Click

  ⌄ next to Decline, choose Reply with Message, type your message, then click Send. Both you and the caller must be signed in to iMessage.

- *Decline a call and set a reminder to call back later:* Click ⌄ next to Decline, then choose how long you want to wait to receive a reminder. When the time comes, you receive a notification—click it to view the reminder, then click the link in the reminder to start the call.

If your Mac has a Touch Bar, you can use it to accept a call, decline a call, decline and send a message, or decline and set a reminder.

You can't receive a call from someone who's restricted by communication limits in Screen Time, but it appears as a missed call in the FaceTime window or in Notification Center.

Manage phone calls in FaceTime on Mac

When you make or receive a phone call in FaceTime, you can manage the call in various ways, such as transferring a call to your iPhone or using call waiting.

Note: Phone calls you make and receive on your Mac use cellular minutes—cellular charges may apply.

- *Switch to a FaceTime video call:* Click Video in the notification (or use the Touch Bar).
- *Switch to an RTT call:* Click RTT in the notification.
  Note: When you switch a phone call to an RTT call, the

  microphone remains active—click the Mute button 🎤 (or use the Touch Bar) to turn off audio for the call.
- *Use call waiting:* If you're on a call and a new phone call

  notification appears, click Hold & Accept. Click ↓∪↑ to switch between calls.
- *Add an incoming caller to a current call:* Click Hold & Accept, wait for the incoming call to connect, then click Merge.
- *Transfer the call to your iPhone:* When your Mac is near your iPhone, swipe up from the bottom to the middle of your iPhone screen and hold until you see the App Switcher. Tap the Phone app banner at the bottom of the screen. Depending on how you set up Wi-Fi Calling, a green bar that says "Touch to return to call" might appear at the top of the screen on your iPhone when you unlock it.
- *Control the volume and other audio options.*

Sync music, books, and more between devices

You can select the information you want to sync between your Mac and device. You can sync all items of a specific type (for example, all your movies or photos). Or you can select specific items (for example, some of your movies and some of your books), which gives you more control.

After you select the content you want to sync, the items are updated whenever you sync your device and your Mac.

The first time you set up syncing, you must connect your device to your Mac using a USB or USB-C cable. After you connect the device, the device icon appears in the Finder sidebar and selecting the icon displays syncing options. You then select which items to sync.

If you have an iPhone (with iOS 5 or later) or iPad, you can also set up to sync wirelessly when your Mac and device are connected to the same Wi-Fi network.

Sync all items of a content type

1. Connect your device to your Mac.
   You can connect your device using a USB or USB-C cable or using a Wi-Fi connection.

2. In the Finder  on your Mac, select the device in the Finder sidebar.

3. Click the type of content you want to sync in the button bar.

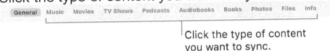

Click the type of content you want to sync.

   Note: If you use iCloud Photos and Apple Music, your photos and music are synced automatically using iCloud. When you click Music or Photos, no options appear for syncing.

4. Select the "Sync [*content type*] onto [*device name*]" checkbox to turn on syncing for that type of item. For example, select the "Sync movies onto [*device name*]" checkbox to sync your movies.

   With the checkbox selected, syncing is set to transfer all items of that type to your device.

5. Repeat steps 3 and 4 for each type of content you want to sync.
   The bar at the bottom of the window shows how much free space remains on your device after you sync. Move the pointer over the bar to view details about the content you're syncing.

147

6. When you're ready to sync, click Apply.

You can choose to sync your Mac and your device automatically whenever you connect them.

WARNING: If you delete an automatically synced item from your Mac, the deleted item is removed from your device the next time you sync.

Before disconnecting your device from your Mac, click the Eject button ⏏ in the Finder sidebar.

Apple ID and iCloud

Manage Apple ID settings

Your Apple ID gives you access to all Apple services, including the App Store, Apple Music, iCloud, iMessage, FaceTime, and more. After you sign in with your Apple ID, you can use Apple ID settings to change your personal information, sign-in and security settings, payment and shipping information, and more.

Apple ID settings showing the user's Apple ID picture and name at the top, and the different types of account options you can set up and use below.

1. On your Mac, choose Apple menu > System Settings, then click [your name] at the top of the sidebar.
   If you don't see your name, click "Sign in with your Apple ID," enter your Apple ID (or a Reachable At email address or phone number that you added in Apple ID settings), then enter your password. If you don't have an Apple ID, you can create one.

2. Click any of the following items on the right to manage the related Apple ID settings on your Mac:
   - **Personal Information**: Use these options to change the photo, name, and birthday associated with your Apple ID.
   - **Sign-In & Security**: Use these options to change the contact information, password, trusted phone numbers, and security settings associated with your Apple ID.
   - **Payment and Shipping**: Use these options to see the payment method or update the shipping address associated with your Apple ID.
   - **iCloud**: Use these options to select the iCloud features you want to use, manage iCloud storage, and set up iCloud+ features.
   - **Media & Purchases**: Use these options to update your account settings, subscriptions, and requirements for downloads and purchases.
   - **Family Sharing**: Use these options to set up and manage a Family Sharing group to share your subscriptions, purchases, location, and more, with up to five family members.

- **Devices**: Use this list to review and manage the trusted devices that use your Apple ID..
- **Sign Out**: Sign out of your Apple ID.
- **About Apple ID & Privacy**: Review information about the Apple Privacy Policy used to protect your Apple ID information.

For information about changing your Apple ID account information on the Apple ID website, see your Apple ID account page.

For information about changing Apple ID account settings using an iOS or iPadOS device, see "Manage Apple ID settings" in the user guide for iPhone, iPad, or iPod touch.

Set your Apple ID picture

You can set a photo, Memoji, emoji, or other image as your Apple ID picture. Your Apple ID picture is also displayed as your user login picture on your Mac and as the picture for your My Card in Contacts.

1. On your Mac, choose Apple menu > System Settings, then click [*your name*] at the top of the sidebar.
   If you don't see your name, click "Sign in with your Apple ID," enter your Apple ID (or a Reachable At email address or phone number that you added in Apple ID settings), then enter your password. If you don't have an Apple ID, you can create one.
2. Click Personal Information on the right.

3. Next to "Memoji, photo, or monogram," click Edit. The Apple ID picture options appear.

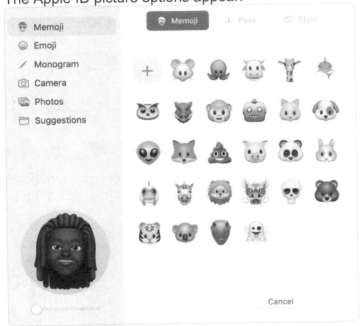

4. Do any of the following:
   - *Select a Memoji:* Click Memoji in the sidebar, then click one of the displayed Memoji or Animoji on the right, or click the Add button ✛ , select and customize facial features and other items such as clothing, then click Done. Click Pose to choose how you want your Memoji or Animoji to pose. Click Style to set a background color.

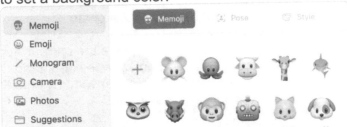

   Tip: Animate your user login picture. Set a Memoji or Animoji as your Apple ID picture and watch as it comes to life every time you log in to your user account.

- *Select an emoji:* Click Emoji in the sidebar, then click one of the displayed emoji on the right, or click the Add button ✛ , then select an emoji. Click Style, then select a background color.

- *Select a monogram:* Click Monogram in the sidebar, select a background color on the right, then enter up to two initials.

- *Take a picture using the camera on your Mac:* Click Camera in the sidebar, set up your shot, then click the Camera button. You can retake the photo as many times as you need to.

- *Select a photo from your Photos library:* Click Photos in the sidebar, then select a photo on the right. To see photos from a specific album, click Albums in the sidebar, then select a photo.

   Tip: To quickly replace the current Apple ID picture with an image on your desktop, drag the image from the desktop or a Finder window onto the current picture in the sidebar.

- ○ *Select a suggested image:* Click Suggestions in the sidebar, then select a picture on the right.

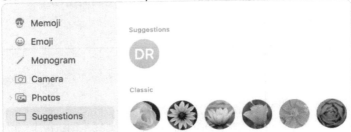

5. After you select an image, you can adjust the way it looks by doing any of the following in the sidebar:
    - ○ *Adjust the image location:* Drag the picture around within the circle.
    - ○ *Zoom in or out:* Drag the slider left or right.
6. When you're done, click Save.

Tip: You can share your Apple ID picture or another picture in the messages you send.

What is iCloud?

iCloud helps you keep your most important information—like your photos, files, and backups—secure, up to date, and available across all your devices. iCloud also makes it easy to share photos, files, notes, and more with friends and family.

iCloud includes a free email account and 5 GB of free storage for your data. For more storage and additional features, you can upgrade to iCloud+.

To get started, sign in with your Apple ID to set up iCloud on your Mac. When you sign in, key features of iCloud like iCloud Photos, iCloud Drive, and more are set up automatically. You can turn these features on or off at any time and customize the settings for each of your devices.

Here are some ways you can use iCloud on your Mac.

iCloud feature	Description
	All your photos and videos. Always available. iCloud Photos securely stores your photos and videos and lets you access them on all your devices and on the web at iCloud.com. With Shared Albums, it's easy to share photos and videos with the people you choose and invite them to add photos, videos, and comments to your shared albums. With iCloud Shared Photo Library, you can collaborate with up to five family members or friends on a shared collection of photos and videos and enjoy more complete memories all in one place.
	Keep all your files securely stored in iCloud Drive Securely store and organize your files in iCloud Drive. Access and keep them up to date across all your devices and on iCloud.com. You can also add your Mac Desktop and Documents folders to iCloud Drive so they're available everywhere. You can share items stored in iCloud and collaborate on them with others. You decide who can view your content and who can make changes. If participants make edits to the content, everyone sees them in real time.
	Share music, books, apps, subscriptions, and more with your family With Family Sharing, you and up to five other family members can share access to amazing Apple

	services like Apple Music, Apple TV+, iCloud+, Apple Fitness+, Apple News+, and Apple Arcade. Your group can also share iTunes, Apple Books, and App Store purchases, an iCloud storage plan, and a family photo album. You can even help locate each other's missing devices. When you subscribe to iCloud+, you can also share all the iCloud+ features and included storage with your family.
	iCloud Private Relay Hide your IP address and browsing activity in Safari and protect your unencrypted internet traffic so that no one—including Apple—can see who you are or what sites you visit. Available with iCloud+.
	Hide My Email Keep your personal email address private by creating unique, random addresses that forward to your personal inbox and can be deleted at any time. Available with iCloud+.
	Your favorite apps are even better with iCloud Keep your mail, calendars, notes, contacts, reminders, messages, and more in sync across all your devices.
	Safari bookmarks, open tabs, Reading List, and Tab Groups Sync your open browser tabs across all your devices, access the same bookmarks, and read articles from your Reading List, even when you're offline. Plus,

	keep your Tab Groups up to date on all your devices, and collaborate on Tab Groups with others.
🔑	*iCloud Keychain* Securely store your passwords, credit cards, and more in iCloud. Autofill your information in Safari and other supported web browsers.
☁	*iCloud storage* Everyone gets 5 GB of free iCloud storage to get started and it's easy to upgrade at any time. Your apps and iTunes Store purchases don't count toward your iCloud storage space, so you only need it for things like photos, videos, files, and device backups. Data stored in iCloud is encrypted, and with two-factor authentication, your account can only be accessed on devices you trust.

iCloud requires an internet connection; some iCloud features have minimum system requirements.

iCloud may not be available in all countries or regions, and iCloud features may vary by area.

What is iCloud+?

iCloud+ gives you everything iCloud offers plus premium features including iCloud Private Relay, Hide My Email, HomeKit Secure Video support, support for custom email domains, and all the storage you need for your data.

- *iCloud Private Relay:* Hide your IP address and browsing activity in Safari and protect your unencrypted internet traffic—without affecting browsing performance.

- *Hide My Email:* With Hide My Email, create unique, random email addresses that forward to your personal inbox so you can send and receive email without having to share your personal email address.
- *HomeKit Secure Video:* Connect your home security cameras in the Home app to record your footage and view it from anywhere, while keeping it private and secure.
- *Custom email domain:* Using iCloud.com, you can purchase a custom email domain or import one you already own and use it with iCloud Mail.
- *iCloud storage:* iCloud+ includes additional iCloud storage. You can choose an iCloud+ plan with 50 GB, 200 GB, 2 TB, 6 TB, or 12 TB of storage.

Subscribe to iCloud+

You can subscribe to iCloud+ or to Apple One, which includes iCloud+ and other services.

Note: iCloud+ may not be available in all countries or regions.

Share iCloud+

When you set up Family Sharing, you can share your iCloud+ subscription with members of your Family Sharing group.

If you join a Family Sharing group that subscribes to iCloud+ or Apple One and you already subscribe, your subscription isn't renewed on your next billing date; instead, you use the group's subscription. If you join a Family Sharing group that doesn't subscribe, the group uses your subscription.

To stop sharing iCloud+ with a Family Sharing group, you can cancel the subscription, leave the group, or stop using Family Sharing.

Change or cancel your iCloud+ subscription

You can change or cancel your iCloud+ subscription using the same procedure you use to manage your iCloud storage plan.

Store files in iCloud Drive

With iCloud Drive, you can safely store all kinds of documents in iCloud, and access them from any of your devices and on the web at iCloud.com.

You can use iCloud Drive on Mac computers (OS X 10.10 or later), iOS devices (iOS 8 or later), iPadOS devices, and Windows computers with iCloud for Windows (Windows 7 or later required). You must be signed in with the same Apple ID on all your devices, and they must meet minimum system requirements.

Note: If you have devices with iCloud Drive turned off, documents and data on those devices aren't kept up to date with documents and data on your devices with iCloud Drive turned on.

Set up iCloud Drive

If you haven't yet set up iCloud Drive on this Mac, you can do it now in iCloud settings.

1. On your Mac, choose Apple menu > System Settings, then click [*your name*] at the top of the sidebar.
    If you don't see your name, click "Sign in with your Apple ID," enter your Apple ID (or a Reachable At email address or phone number that you added in Apple ID settings), then enter your password. If you don't have an Apple ID, you can create one.
2. Click iCloud on the right, click iCloud Drive, then turn on Sync this Mac.
3. Click Done.

Store your Desktop and Documents folders in iCloud Drive

You can have all the files in your Desktop and Documents folders stored automatically in iCloud Drive. That way, you can save files right where you usually keep them, and they become available on all your devices and iCloud.com.

1. On your Mac, choose Apple menu > System Settings, then click [*your name*] at the top of the sidebar.
   If you don't see your name, click "Sign in with your Apple ID," enter your Apple ID (or a Reachable At email address or phone number that you added in Apple ID settings), then enter your password. If you don't have an Apple ID, you can create one.
2. Click iCloud on the right, click iCloud Drive, then make sure iCloud Drive is turned on.
3. Turn on Desktop & Documents Folders.
4. Click Done.

After you turn on Desktop & Documents Folders, your Desktop and Documents folders are moved into iCloud Drive. They also appear in the iCloud section of the Finder sidebar on your Mac, and in the Files app on your iPhone or iPad.

Tip: You can quickly view the sync status of iCloud Drive on your Mac. Move the pointer over iCloud Drive in the Finder sidebar, then click the status or information icon.

If you can't move or save a document to iCloud Drive

If you can't move or save a document to iCloud Drive, your iCloud storage space may be full. The document stays on your Mac, and is uploaded to iCloud Drive when space becomes available.

iCloud Drive shares your iCloud storage with iCloud Photos, iOS and iPadOS device backups, messages and attachments in iCloud Mail, and more.

To get more space, do the following:

- Upgrade your storage.
- Remove items you don't need to store in iCloud Drive.

Share and collaborate on files and folders

You can use iCloud Drive to share files and folders with others so you can collaborate on projects together. The people you invite can download the shared items from iCloud to any of their devices, where they can view them and—depending on the privileges you set—collaborate. You can see any updates the next time you open the files on your Mac.

Note: To use iCloud Drive folder sharing, your computer or device must have macOS version 10.15.4 or later, iOS version 13.4 or later, or iCloud for Windows version 11.1 or later.

Tip: You can also collaborate on shared content directly from supported apps like Notes, Reminders, Safari, Keynote, Pages, Numbers, and more, as long as you set up iCloud for that app.

Invite people to collaborate on files or folders

1. To invite people to collaborate on files or folders, do one of the following on your Mac:
   ○ Click the Finder icon in the Dock to open a Finder window, click iCloud Drive in the sidebar, select a file or folder, then click the Share button.
   ○ Control-click an item on the desktop, then choose Share from the shortcut menu.
2. *Note:* To collaborate with others on a file or folder, it must be in iCloud Drive.
3. Choose Collaborate from the pop-up menu.

4. Click "Only invited people can edit." below Collaborate to set permissions for working together, then choose one of the following from the pop-up menu below "Who can access":
   ○ *Only invited people:* Allow only people you invite to access the file or folder.

- *Anyone with the link:* Allow anyone who receives the link to access the file or folder. If you choose this option, people you invite can share the link and give access to others not included in your original invitation.
5. Click the pop-up menu below Permissions, then choose one of the following:
    - *Can make changes:* Allow people you invite to view and modify the contents of the file or folder.
    - *View only:* Allow people you invite to view the contents of the file or folder, but not modify them.
6. Select the checkbox next to "Allow others to invite" to allow anyone with access to the file or folder to share it with others. Deselect the checkbox so only you can share the file or folder with others.
7. Share the invitation using Mail or Messages, or create and copy a link to the shared item.

When the people you invite receive your invitation, they can download the shared file or folder from iCloud to any of their devices. If you allow it, they can make changes to a file, and you see the updates the next time you open it on your Mac.

When you share a folder with only invited people, only they can access the files in the shared folder. To add more participants, you must change the settings of the shared folder; you can't change the settings of an individual file within the folder.

Tip: If you want to send a copy of a file or folder without collaborating on it, Control-click the item in the Finder or on the desktop, choose Share from the shortcut menu, choose Send Copy from the pop-up menu, then choose how you want to share the copy of the item, such as using AirDrop or Mail.

Accept an invitation to a shared file or folder

- On your Mac, click the link you received to the shared item, then click Open to view the item in the Finder and have it added to iCloud Drive.

When you accept an invitation to a shared file or folder, it's available in the following locations:

- In iCloud Drive on your Mac
- The Files app on your iOS or iPadOS device (iOS 11 or later)
- On iCloud.com
- On a PC with iCloud for Windows

You can open the shared item with any compatible app and make changes, if you have permission to edit. Anyone with access to the item sees the latest changes the next time they open it.

Change the sharing settings of a file or folder

You can change the sharing settings of a file or folder you share at any time.

Note: You can't change the sharing settings for an individual document in a shared folder. You must change the settings of the folder.

1. On your Mac, click the Finder icon 😊 in the Dock to open a Finder window, then click iCloud Drive in the sidebar.
2. Control-click the file or folder, then choose Manage Shared File or Manage Shared Folder.
3. Do any of the following:
   - *Share an item with more people:* Click the Add button ➕.
   - *Copy a link to the shared item to send to another person:* Click Copy Link. You can paste the link into a message, email, or other app.
   - *Change who can access the file to download:* Click the pop-up menu on the left below Permissions, then choose "Only people you invite" to only allow people you invite to access the item, or choose "Anyone with the link" to allow anyone who receives the link to access the item.
   - *Change whether the shared document can be modified or only viewed:* Click the pop-up menu on the right below Permissions, then choose "can make changes" to allow others to revise the document, or choose "can view only" to allow read-only access.

162

○ *Change who can invite more people:* Select "Anyone can add more people" to allow anyone who can access the item to invite others. If you don't select this option, only you can invite others.

○ *Change the sharing settings for a specific person:*

Move the pointer over a person's name, click ⋯, then choose the settings you want.

○ *Stop sharing a file with a specific person:* Position the pointer over the person's name, click ⋯, then choose Remove Access.

4. Click Done.

View and manage your shared files

You can use the Shared folder in the Finder sidebar to easily view files and folders shared by others and by you. To set up your Shared folder to display folders grouped by who shared them, do the following:

1. On your Mac, click the Finder icon 🙂 in the Dock to open a Finder window, then click Shared in the sidebar.
2. Click the Grouping pop-up menu in the toolbar, then choose Shared By.

The window displays the files and folders shared by you and

others, grouped by the person sharing them.

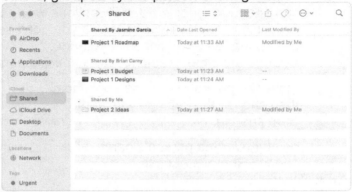

Stop sharing a file or folder

1. On your Mac, click the Finder icon ![Finder] in the Dock to open a Finder window, then click iCloud Drive in the sidebar.
2. Control-click the item, then choose Manage Shared File or Manage Shared Folder.
3. Do any of the following:
   o *Stop sharing with everyone:* Click Stop Sharing.
   o *Stop sharing with a specific person:* Move the pointer over the person's name, click ^{•••}, then choose Remove Access.

You can also simply move the file or folder out of iCloud Drive or delete it to stop others from having access to it.

If you stop sharing or delete a shared folder, the files in the folder are no longer accessible to the participants.

Note: If anyone you share with makes their own copy of the item, they can continue to access their copy even after you stop sharing yours.

Manage iCloud storage

When you sign in with your Apple ID and turn on iCloud, you automatically get 5 GB of free storage. You can use your iCloud storage for photos, files, backups, and more. You can increase your storage by upgrading to iCloud+.

You can also remove items stored in iCloud to make more space available.

View and manage iCloud storage

1. On your Mac, choose Apple menu > System Settings, then click [your name] at the top of the sidebar.
   If you don't see your name, click "Sign in with your Apple ID," enter your Apple ID (or a Reachable At email address or phone number that you added in Apple ID settings), then enter your password. If you don't have an Apple ID, you can create one.
2. Click iCloud on the right, click Manage, then do any of the following:
   - *Upgrade your storage:* Click Change Storage Plan or Add Storage, then follow the onscreen instructions.
   - *Share iCloud+ with your Family:* If you subscribe to iCloud+, click Share with Family, then follow the onscreen instructions.
     If Share with Family isn't shown, you can share iCloud+ with your family in Family Sharing settings.
     Note: If you're in a Family Sharing group and you use the same Apple ID to share family purchases, the storage upgrade is billed to the family organizer's account.
   - *See how an app or feature is using storage:* Click an app or feature in the list.
     You can permanently remove all documents and data for an app. You can save copies of documents before removing them from iCloud.
   - *Remove an iOS or iPadOS device backup:* Click Backups in the list, select a device whose backup you don't need, then click Remove ⎯ (below the list of backups).
     WARNING: If you delete the iCloud backup for your current iOS or iPadOS device, iCloud stops automatically backing up the device.

165

- *Turn off Siri and remove Siri-related data:* Click Siri in the list, then click Disable and Delete.

3. Click Done.

iCloud+ may not be available in all countries or regions, and iCloud+ features may vary by area.

Use iCloud Photos

With iCloud Photos, all the photos and videos in your photo library are stored in iCloud, so you can access them from your Mac, PC, iPhone, iPad, or Apple TV, and on iCloud.com.

Any new photos and videos you add to Photos appear on all your devices that have iCloud Photos turned on. Your photos and albums are organized the same way on every device, and if you make edits or remove items, the changes appear on all your devices. When you get a new device, iCloud Photos quickly syncs your photo library to it.

Before you begin

- *Make sure your Mac and other devices have the latest software:* Update to the latest version of macOS on your Mac, or iOS or iPadOS on your iPhone or iPad.
- *Sign in with your Apple ID:* If you're not signed in with your Apple ID, choose Apple menu > System Settings, then click "Sign in with your Apple ID" at the top of the sidebar. Enter your Apple ID or create one. Click iCloud on the right, click Photos in the list of apps, then turn on Sync this Mac.

Turn on iCloud Photos

1. In the Photos app on your Mac, choose Photos > Settings, then click iCloud.

2. Select the iCloud Photos checkbox.

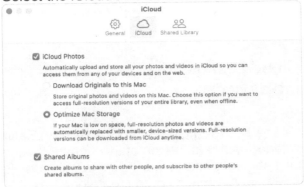

3. Select one of the following options:
   - *Download Originals to this Mac:* Stores the full-size versions of your photos both on your Mac and in iCloud.
   - *Optimize Mac Storage:* Stores smaller versions of your photos on your Mac when storage space is limited, and keeps the original, full-size photos in iCloud. Choose this option to conserve space on your Mac. To restore the originals to your Mac, just select "Download Originals to this Mac."

When you first turn on iCloud Photos, it can take a while to upload your photos to iCloud. You can continue to use Photos while your photos are being uploaded.

To have iCloud Photos sync photos to all your devices, use the same Apple ID to turn on iCloud Photos on all your devices.

Stop using iCloud Photos on a Mac

You can turn off iCloud Photos on your Mac so that photos aren't updated between your Mac and your other devices.

1. In the Photos app on your Mac, choose Photos > Settings, then click iCloud.
2. Deselect the iCloud Photos checkbox.
3. Click Download to download photos and videos from iCloud to your Mac, or click Remove from Mac to remove any photos and videos that have not been fully downloaded.

After you turn off iCloud Photos on your Mac, your photo library remains in iCloud and available to your other devices that use iCloud Photos.

Stop using iCloud Photos on all your Apple computers and devices

1. On your Mac, choose Apple menu > System Settings, then click [*your name*] at the top of the sidebar.
   If you don't see your name, click "Sign in with your Apple ID" to sign in with your Apple ID or to create one.
2. Click iCloud on the right.
3. Click the Manage button, click Photos, then click "Turn Off and Delete."

WARNING: If you turn off iCloud Photos on all your devices, your photos and videos will be deleted from iCloud in 30 days, and you won't be able to recover them, unless you click Undo Delete before that time.

Family and friends

What is Family Sharing?

With Family Sharing, you and up to five other family members can share subscriptions to Apple services like Apple Music, Apple TV+, iCloud+, Apple Fitness+, Apple News+, and Apple Arcade. Your family group can also share iTunes Store, App Store, and Apple Books purchases, an iCloud storage plan, and a family photo album. You can even help locate each other's missing devices.

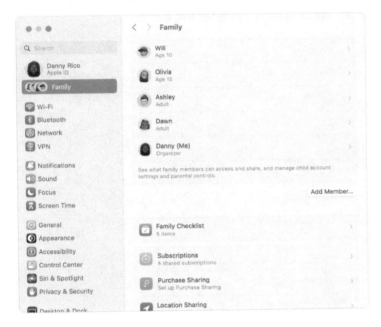

One adult—the family organizer—sets up Family Sharing, invites up to five family members to join the group, and chooses the features the family can share. When family members join, they have instant access to the shared content.

Each family member needs an Apple ID and must be signed in with their Apple ID to access Family settings. The organizer, a parent, or a guardian can add a child to the group and create an Apple ID for them.

Note: Family Sharing is designed to be used by a single family (adults and children). You can be part of only one Family Sharing group at a time.

Family Sharing is available on Mac computers (OS X 10.10 or later), iOS devices (iOS 8 or later), iPadOS devices, and Windows computers with iCloud for Windows (Windows 7 or later required).

Set up Family Sharing

To set up Family Sharing, one adult—the family organizer—invites family members to join the Family Sharing group. Each family member needs an Apple ID to participate in the group.

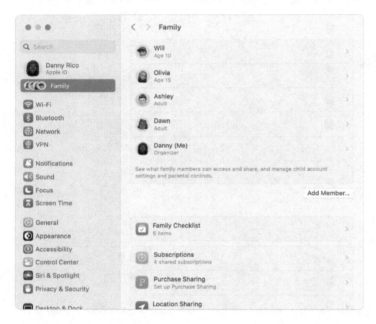

1. On your Mac, choose Apple menu > System Settings, then click [*your name*] at the top of the sidebar.
   If you don't see your name, click "Sign in with your Apple ID," enter your Apple ID (or a Reachable At email address or phone number that you added in Apple ID settings), then enter your password. If you don't have an Apple ID, you can create one.
2. Click Family Sharing on the right, click Set Up Family, then invite people to join your Family Sharing group:

- *Invite family members:* Click Invite People, then follow the onscreen instructions.

  If the person you're inviting is nearby, you can choose Invite in Person and ask them to enter their Apple ID and password on your Mac. Otherwise, you can send the invitation using Mail, Messages, or AirDrop.

  If the person you're inviting doesn't have an Apple ID, they have to create one before they can accept your invitation.
- *Create an Apple ID for a younger child:* Click Create Child Account, then follow the onscreen instructions.

3. To add more family members to your Family Sharing group, click Add Member, then follow the onscreen instructions.
4. Do any of the following:
   - *Complete suggested tasks:* Click Family Checklist. You see a list of suggestions for getting the most out of Family Sharing. For example, you can set up parental controls for kids, share your location, or add a recovery contact.
   - *Find subscription services to share:* Click Subscriptions. You see a list of services you subscribe to that are available to share. Click the name of the subscription, then follow the onscreen instructions to share with your family.

     Apple subscriptions, except iCloud+, are automatically shared with your family. You can choose to share iCloud+, or family members can choose to keep their own individual storage plans.

     To learn about other Apple subscriptions, click Apple Subscriptions or the name of a service below Discover More. To explore more family subscriptions in the App Store, click Discover next to Subscriptions for Family.
   - *Set up purchase sharing:* Click Purchase Sharing, click Continue, then click Turn On Purchase Sharing. Your family can share purchases from the iTunes Store, App Store, and Apple Books, so everyone has access to them. All purchases are made through the shared payment method you set up.
   - *Set up location sharing:* Click Location Sharing, then turn location sharing or for each family member you want to share your location with. Turn on

Automatically Share Location to automatically share your location with any new family members who join later. You can set up location sharing so that all family members can view each other's locations in the Find My and Messages apps. You can use the Find My app on your Mac, iOS device, and iPadOS device, and on iCloud.com.

o *Set up Ask To Buy:* Click the name of a child in your Family Sharing group, click Ask To Buy in the sidebar, then click Turn On Ask to Buy. This setting requires children in your Family Sharing group to get your approval to download or purchase items from the App Store, iTunes Store, or Apple Books.
Age restrictions for Ask to Buy vary by area. In the United States, the family organizer can turn on Ask to Buy for any family member under age 18; for children under age 13, it's on by default.

o *Set up Screen Time and parental controls:* Click the name of the family member, click Screen Time in the sidebar, click Open [*family member's*] Screen Time, then select the options you want.
Age restrictions for Screen Time vary by area. In the United States, the family organizer can turn on Screen Time for any family member under age 18.

Set up Screen Time for a child

The most flexible and convenient way to set up and manage Screen Time for a child is by using Family Sharing. When you use Family Sharing, you can remotely manage and monitor each child's device usage from your own account on any Mac, iPhone, or iPad. However, if you aren't using Family Sharing, you can still set up Screen Time for a child by logging in to their Mac account.

Note: For children under 13, Communication Safety and Screen Distance are turned on by default, and the Web Content Filter blocks adult content.

Family Member   Will Rico ↕

Activity

📊 App & Website Activity   >

🔔 Notifications   >

📱 Pickups   >

Limit Usage

⏲ Downtime   >

⏳ App Limits   >

✓ Always Allowed   >

A Screen Distance   >

Communication

💬 Communication Limits   >

💬 Communication Safety   >

1. On your Mac, do one of the following:
   - *If you're using Family Sharing:* Log in to your Mac user account, then make sure you're signed in with your Apple ID.
   - *If you aren't using Family Sharing:* Log in to the child's Mac user account.

2. Choose Apple menu > System Settings, then click Screen Time ⧖ in the sidebar. (You may need to scroll down.)

3. If you're using Family Sharing, click the pop-up menu on the right, then choose a child.

4. Click Set Up Screen Time For Your Child, click Turn on Screen Time, then follow the onscreen instructions.
   During the setup process, you can set content restrictions, turn on Screen Distance, turn on App & Website Activity, set time away from screens, and create a 4-digit Screen Time passcode.

5. In Screen Time settings, scroll down, then turn on any of the following options:
   - *Include Website Data:* Turn on this option if you want Screen Time reports to include details about the

specific websites visited. If you don't turn on this option, websites are just reported as Safari usage.

- o *Lock Screen Time Settings:* Turn on this option to require a passcode to access Screen Time settings and allow additional time when limits expire.
Note: If the family member has an administrator account, you're prompted to convert it to a standard account.

6. You can also do any of the following in Screen Time settings:
   - o Click App & Website Activity, Notifications, or Pickups, then view your app and device usage.
   - o Click Downtime, then set up a downtime schedule.
   - o Click App Limits, then set time limits for apps and websites.
   - o Click Always Allowed, then choose apps that can be used at any time.
   - o Click Screen Distance, then receive alerts when you're holding a device too close.
   - o Click Communication Limits, then set communication limits.
   - o Click Communication Safety, then choose to check for sensitive photos.
   - o Click Content & Privacy, then set up content & privacy restrictions.

Share purchases with your family

As a member of a Family Sharing group, you have immediate access to purchases shared by other group members. You can download their purchases on your Mac, iOS device, and iPadOS device at any time.

Other members of the group can access your purchases in the same way. You can hide individual purchases you don't want other group members to share.

Only the family organizer can set up purchase sharing.

View and download purchases made by other family members

The way you download purchases made by other family members varies depending on the app.

- *View or download music:* Sign in to the Music app 🎵 on your Mac, then choose Account > Purchased. Click the pop-up menu next to Purchased, choose a family member, then download the items you want.

- *View or download apps:* Sign in to the App Store app 🅰 on your Mac, then choose Store > Account. Click the "Purchased by" pop-up menu, choose a family member, then download the items you want.

- *View or download books:* Sign in to the Books app 📖 on your Mac, then choose Account > View My Account. Below Family Purchases, click a family member, then download the items you want.

When a family member initiates a purchase, it's billed directly to the family organizer's account. After it's purchased, the item is added to the initiating family member's account and is shared with the rest of the group. If the family organizer ever stops Family Sharing, each person keeps the items they chose to purchase—even if they were paid for by the family organizer.

Hide a purchase from other family members

You can hide your individual Music, App Store, and Apple Books purchases so they aren't available to other family members.

- *Hide music:* Sign in to the Music app 🎵 on your Mac, then choose Account > Purchased. Select the type of content you want to hide, place the pointer over the item you want to hide, click the Delete button ✕ , then click Hide.

- *Hide apps:* Sign in to the App Store app 🅰 on your Mac, then choose Store > Account. Move the pointer over the app you want to hide, click the More Options button ⋯ , choose Hide Purchase, then click Hide Purchase.

- *Hide books:* Sign in to the Books app 📖 on your Mac, then click All (or another collection) in the sidebar. Click the More

Options button ⁝⁝⁝ below the item you want to hide, click Remove, then click Hide *<item type>*.

Stop hiding a purchase

You can reveal individual Music, App Store, and Apple Books purchases that you hid previously so they're available to other family members.

- *Stop hiding music:* Sign in to the Music app on your Mac, then choose Account > Account Settings. Go to Downloads and Purchases, click Manage, then click Unhide for the item.

- *Stop hiding apps:* Sign in to the App Store app on your Mac, then choose Store > Account. Click Account Settings. In the hidden items section, click Manage, then click Unhide for the item.

- *Stop hiding books:* Sign in to the Books app on your Mac, then choose Account > View My Account. Click Manage Hidden Purchases, enter your Apple ID and password, click Sign In, then click Unhide for the item.

Stop sharing your purchases

When you stop sharing your purchases, your family members lose access to all your shared iTunes Store, App Store, and Apple Books purchases.

1. On your Mac, choose Apple menu > System Settings, then click Family in the sidebar.
   If you don't see Family, set up Family Sharing.
2. Click Purchase Sharing on the right, click [*your name*], then turn off Share My Purchases.

Turn off purchase sharing

When you turn off purchase sharing for your Family Sharing group, your family members lose access to all shared iTunes Store, App

Store, and Apple Books purchases and can't make new shared purchases.

Only the family organizer can turn off purchase sharing for the group.

1. On your Mac, choose Apple menu > System Settings, then click Family in the sidebar.
   If you don't see Family, set up Family Sharing.
2. Click Purchase Sharing on the right, click Stop Purchase Sharing, then click Stop Purchase Sharing again.

Note: To share purchases, family members must be in the same iTunes Store country or region. If a family member changes their iTunes Store country or region, that person might lose access to other family members' purchases, and installed apps that were shared from other family members might not work.

Watch and listen together with SharePlay

With macOS 12 or later, you can use SharePlay in FaceTime to bring TV shows, movies, and music into your video calls. With simultaneous playback and shared controls, you can enjoy a real-time connection with everyone on the call—you all see and hear the same moments at the same time. With smart volume, audio is adjusted automatically, so you can continue to chat while watching or listening.

Note: Some apps that support SharePlay require a subscription to participate. Not all features and content are available in all countries or regions.

Watch video together

You can watch TV shows and movies during a FaceTime call with others. If everyone on the call has access to the video content (by subscription or free trial, for example), they can see the same moments at the same time, and use the shared playback controls to press Play or Pause. The show or movie volume adjusts automatically so you can keep talking while you watch.

- While on a FaceTime call on your Mac, start watching a movie or show in the Apple TV app .
  If this is the first time you're using SharePlay, confirm that you want to use it. From then on, SharePlay starts automatically. If you select Start Only for Me, you're asked the next time you want to use SharePlay for the Apple TV app.

Everyone on the call who has access to the content can watch at the same time. People who don't have access are asked to get access (through a subscription, a transaction, or a free trial, if available).

While watching together, everyone can use playback controls on their respective Apple devices to play, pause, rewind, or fast-forward in real time.

Tip: You can arrange windows so that you see the FaceTime video call on one side of your screen and the movie or show on the other side.

Listen to music together

You can get together and listen to music with others on a FaceTime call. If everyone on the call has the required access to the music, they can hear the song at the same time, see the name of the song and what's up next, and use the shared controls to pause playback, reorder songs, add songs to the queue, and jump to the next track. The music volume adjusts automatically so you can keep talking while you listen.

1. While on a FaceTime call on your Mac, move the pointer over any song or album in the Music app , then click the Play button to start the music.
   If this is the first time you're using SharePlay, confirm that you want to use it. From then on, SharePlay starts automatically. If you select Start Only for Me, you're asked the next time you want to use SharePlay for Music.
   Everyone on the call who has access to the content hears the music start playing at the same time. People who don't

have access are asked to get access (through a subscription, a transaction, or a free trial, if available).
2. While listening together, anyone on the call can control the playback (pause the music, go to the next song, and more), manage the shared Playing Next queue, and view lyrics.

Continue watching on your Apple TV

While using SharePlay, you can send a video, show, or movie that you're watching to an Apple TV.

Share a Photo Library

iCloud Shared Photo Library lets you and up to five family members or friends collaborate on a photo collection, so you can enjoy more complete memories, all in one place. You can belong to one Shared Library at a time.

When you set up or join a Shared Library, the photos and videos you contribute move from your Personal Library to the Shared Library, and all members of the Shared Library can view, edit, and delete them.

What you need to use iCloud Shared Photo Library

You can invite family members or friends who have a Mac with macOS 13 or later, or an iPhone or iPad with a version of iOS 16 or iPadOS 16 that supports iCloud Shared Photo Library. Participants must have an Apple ID and have turned on iCloud Photos on their Mac or other devices. Children under 13 must be part of the organizer's iCloud Family Sharing group.

Participants can access the Shared Library from their Mac, iPhone, iPad, Apple TV, PC, and iCloud.com.

Set up a Shared Library

1. In the Photos app on your Mac, choose Photos > Settings, click Shared Library, then click Get Started.

2. Click Add Participants ⊕, enter the name of a family member or friend that you want to invite to join the Shared Library, click the name to select it, then click Add.
   You can repeat this step to invite up to five participants.
3. Click Continue.
4. To move photos to the Shared Library, click an option:
   - *All My Photos and Videos:* Move all your existing photos and videos to the Shared Library. Click Next, then follow the onscreen instructions.
     Note: Screenshots, screen recordings, and hidden items are not moved to the Shared Library.
   - *Choose by People or Date:* Move photos and videos that include specific people or that were taken after a certain date. Click Next, click Add Other People ⊕, select people, then click Add. Click Skip to add photos by date. Follow the onscreen instructions to set a starting date for photos you want included.
     Tip: When you select a specific person, you can choose to add them to your contacts. This lets Photos create sharing suggestions for future photos you take of that person.
   - *Choose Manually:* Select the photos and videos you want to move to the Shared Library.
5. If you don't want to add items to the Shared Library at this time, click Move Photos Later, then click Next.
6. Click Preview Shared Library to preview the contents of the Shared Library, or click Skip.
   After previewing the Shared Library, click Continue.
7. Click Invite via Messages to send text invitations to participants, or click Copy Link and paste the link into emails that you can send to participants.
8. Click Done.
   Your new Shared Library appears in the Photos window. The Library pop-up menu appears in the toolbar and lets you choose between viewing the Shared Library, your Personal Library, or both libraries at once.

Join a Shared Library

After you accept an invitation to join a Shared Library, you can view, edit, add, favorite, caption, and delete items in the Shared Library.

- In the invitation email or text message, click Shared Library Invitation, then follow the onscreen instructions.
  When you accept the invitation, you can add your own photos to the Shared Library.

Note: The Shared Library organizer provides the storage space for all items in the Shared Library. If the Shared Library content exceeds your available storage space, you can upgrade to iCloud+ or add additional storage to your existing iCloud+ subscription.

Add or remove Shared Library participants

If you're the organizer of a Shared Library, you can add and remove participants.

1. In the Photos app 🌸 on your Mac, choose Photos > Settings, then click Shared Library.
2. Do any of the following:
   - *Add participants:* Click Add Participants, type the name of a family member or friend with an Apple ID, click the name to select it, then click Add.
     People you add receive an email inviting them to join the Shared Library. You can repeat this step to add up to five people. To resend an invitation, click the More button ⋯ next to someone you've added, then choose Resend Invitation.
   - *Remove participants:* Click the More button ⋯ next to the person you want to remove, choose Remove, then click Remove from Shared Library.
     People you remove receive a notification and can copy all of the items in the Shared Library to their Personal Library. (If you remove someone who has been a member of the Shared Library for less than 7 days, they can only retrieve the items they contributed.)

Leave or delete a Shared Library

Participants can choose to leave a Shared Library at any time. If you're the organizer of a Shared Library, you can delete it. When

181

you delete the Shared Library, all participants receive a notification and can choose to keep all of the items in the Shared Library in their Personal Library.

If you leave a Shared Library less than 7 days after joining, you can only keep the items you contributed.

1. In the Photos app on your Mac, choose Photos > Settings, then click Shared Library.
2. Click Leave Shared Library (if you're a participant) or Delete Shared Library (if you're the organizer).
3. Select one of the following options:
    o   *Keep everything:* Add all the photos in the Shared Library to your Personal Library.
    o   *Keep only what I contributed:* Add only photos that you contributed to the Shared Library to your Personal Library.
4. Click Delete Shared Library.
5. Click Delete Shared Library again to confirm the deletion.

Collaborate on projects

You can send an invitation to collaborate on a project in Messages, and everyone in the conversation is automatically added to the document, spreadsheet, or other shared file. When someone makes an edit, you see activity updates at the top of the Messages conversation. Click the updates to get back to the shared content.

Note: To start collaborating on a project with Messages, you and your recipients must be using iMessage on macOS 13 or later, iOS 16 or later, or iPadOS 16.1 or later, and you must first save the content somewhere it can be accessed by others, such as iCloud Drive. For macOS apps, you need to turn on the iCloud features for each app before you can collaborate.

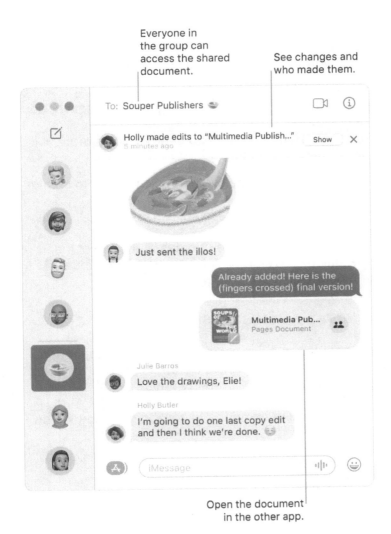

Everyone in the group can access the shared document.

See changes and who made them.

Open the document in the other app.

Drag a file into a Messages conversation to start collaborating

When you're in an individual or group conversation and you want to collaborate, you can add files and folders from iCloud Drive, Keynote, Numbers, and Pages directly into that conversation.

1. In the Finder 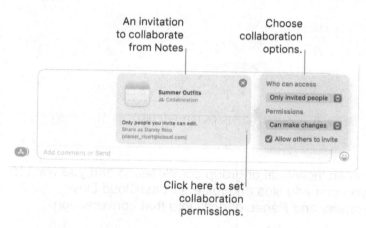 or from your desktop on your Mac, drag a file or folder you want to share to a conversation in the Messages app .
2. In the field at the bottom of the Messages conversation, do any of the following:
   ○ Click the pop-up menu and choose Collaborate, if it isn't already chosen.
   ○ Click the arrow ╱ below the pop-up menu to change the sharing options.
3. Press Return to send the message.

When someone edits the file, you see updates at the top of the Messages conversation. To return to the shared project and see changes, click an update.

Start collaborating in Messages from another app

You can also collaborate on a project when you're in another app, including the Finder, Reminders, Notes, Safari, Freeform, Keynote, Numbers, Pages, and supported third-party apps.

Note: The process for inviting someone to collaborate depends on the app.

An invitation to collaborate from Notes

Choose collaboration options.

Summer Outfits
Collaboration

Only people you invite can edit.
Share as Danny Rico
(daniel_rico1@icloud.com)

Add comment or Send

Who can access

Only invited people

Permissions

Can make changes

☑ Allow others to invite

Click here to set collaboration permissions.

1. In the other app on your Mac, select the file or item you want to share, then click the Share button ⬆.

184

2. Make sure Collaborate is chosen in the pop-up menu, then click Messages. In the To field, type the name, email address, or phone number for every person you want to send the project to.
Optionally, you can choose one of your recent Messages conversations to automatically send to that person or group.
3. In the field at the bottom of the Messages conversation, do any of the following:
    o Click the pop-up menu and choose Collaborate, if it isn't already chosen.
    o Click the arrow ⟩ below the pop-up menu to change the sharing options.
4. Press Return to send the message.

After you invite participants in Messages, you can work on the project in the other app and return to the Messages conversation at any time. Click the Collaborate button (it looks like this 🔵 when there's no photo associated with the conversation; otherwise, you see the individual photo or group icon). Then click the Message button ⬤. Or, quickly start a FaceTime call—just click the Collaborate button, then the Audio button 📞 (for an audio call) or the Video button 🎥 (for a video call).

Manage a project in Messages

After you share a project in an individual or group Messages conversation, you can do any of the following in the Messages app 💬 on your Mac:

- *Go to a project:* In the conversation, click the shared project. Or click the Info button ⓘ in the top-right corner of a conversation, scroll to Collaboration, then click the shared project.
  Tip: If you don't see the shared project you want below Collaboration, click Show More on the right.
- *See project changes and who made them:* At the top of the conversation, click Show or Review whenever someone makes an edit.

185

- *Add a person to a project:* When you're collaborating on a project with a group, you can add people to the group conversation the same way you usually do. Then, grant them access to the project—click Review at the top of the transcript.
- *Remove a person from a project:* When you're collaborating on a project with a group, you can remove people from the group conversation the same way you usually do. Then, make sure to check the participant access in the app (for example, Notes or Pages) to remove viewing or editing privileges.
- *Pin a project:* In the conversation, Control-click the shared project, then choose Pin.
- *Hide a project:* Click the Info button ⓘ in the top-right corner of a conversation, scroll to Collaboration, then Control-click the shared project and choose Hide.
  When you hide a project, it no longer appears below Collaboration (but does appear in the Links section). Hiding a project doesn't remove your sharing privileges or remove you from the collaboration. You can still access the project from the app it's shared in.
- *Share a project:* Click the Info button ⓘ in the top-right corner of a conversation, scroll to Collaboration, then Control-click the shared project and choose Share.
  When you share the project, you can share it with new participants or the same group.

If you Control-click a shared project in the conversation, you can also do any of the following:

- Add a Tapback to it.
- Reply to it.
- Forward it.
- Delete it.

Manage a project in another app

After you share a project in an individual or group Messages conversation, you can make collaboration changes (such as adding new participants, removing participants, or stopping the collaboration) in the other app on your Mac:

- *iCloud Drive in the Finder:* In the Finder app ⬛ on your Mac, select a file or folder you shared from iCloud Drive, Control-click it, then choose Manage Shared File.

- *Reminders:* In the Reminders app ⬛ on your Mac, select a list you shared, then click the Collaborate button.

- *Notes:* In the Notes app ⬛ on your Mac, select a note or folder you shared, then click the Collaborate button.

- *Safari:* In the Safari app ⬛ on your Mac, select a Tab Group you shared, then click the Collaborate button.

- *Freeform (macOS 13.1 or later):* In the Freeform app ⬛ on your Mac, click Shared in the sidebar, double-click a board, then click the Collaborate button.

Note: The group of people in the Messages collaboration and the group collaborating on the project may not match. For instance, you may invite people to collaborate on the file outside of Messages. Or you may have two different groups in Messages, each with its own collaboration conversation.

Find content shared with you

With macOS 12 or later, when a person shares content with you in Messages, such as a link to a news story or TV show, you can find that content in a Shared with You section in the corresponding app. This allows you to view the content at a time that's convenient for you.

Shared with You is available in the following apps: the Apple TV app, Books, Finder, Freeform (macOS 13.1 or later), News, Notes, Photos, Podcasts, Reminders, Safari, iWork apps, and some third-party apps.

Note: Content only appears in Shared with You if the person who sent it is in your contacts.

Turn Shared with You settings on or off

Use Messages settings to choose whether content shared with you appears in the Shared with You section of all available apps or only specific apps.

1. In the Messages app ⬜ on your Mac, choose Messages > Settings, then click Shared with You.
2. Do any of the following:
   - *Turn on all apps:* Click Turn On.
   - *Turn off all apps:* Click Turn Off.
   - *Turn on for selected apps:* Select apps. (Content sent to you with Messages will automatically appear in a Shared with You section in those apps.)
   - *Turn off for selected apps:* Deselect apps.

Turn Shared with You on or off by conversation

You can choose to have content shared in a Messages conversation appear in the Shared with You section of the corresponding app.

1. In the Messages app ⬜ on your Mac, select a conversation.
2. Click the Info button ⓘ in the top-right corner of a conversation, then select Show in Shared with You (or deselect to remove shared content from the Shared with You section).
   When Shared with You is turned off, you can still pin shared content to show it in the corresponding app.

Share content with others

Content you share with others in Messages is automatically organized in a Shared with You section in the corresponding app on their device.

1. Select the content you want to share, click ⬆ or choose Share, then choose Messages.
2. In the To field, type the name, email address, or phone number of the person you want to send the content to. As you type, Messages suggests matching addresses from your

Contacts app ⬤ or from people you've previously sent messages to.

You can also click the Add button ⊕ to the right of the To field. Select a contact in the list, then click the email address or phone number.
Note: If you're restricted to sending and receiving messages with only certain people, an hourglass icon ⧖ appears next to those people you can't send messages to.

3. To include a message with the content, enter it in the field below the link. You can use typing suggestions, if available.
4. Click Send.

See what others have shared with you

You can see what others have shared with you in your Messages conversation, or see it later in the corresponding apps:

- *Apple TV app:* In the Apple TV app 📺 on your Mac, click Watch Now, then scroll down to the Shared with You row.

- *Books:* In the Books app 📖 on your Mac, click Reading Now in the sidebar, then scroll down to Shared with You.

- *Finder:* In the Finder 🙂 on your Mac, click Shared in the sidebar.

- *Freeform (macOS 13.1 or later):* In the Freeform app 〰 on your Mac, click Shared in the sidebar.

- *News:* In the News app ◤ on your Mac, click Shared with You in the sidebar.

- *Notes:* In the Notes app ▢ on your Mac, click Shared in the sidebar.

- *Photos:* In the Photos app ❀ on your Mac, click Shared with You in the sidebar.

- *Podcasts:* In the Podcasts app 🎙 on your Mac, click Listen Now in the sidebar, then go to the Shared with You section.

- *Reminders:* In the Reminders app ☰ on your Mac, click Shared in the sidebar.

- *Safari:* In the Safari app ⬤ on your Mac, click Shared with You in the sidebar.

Continue the conversation

Content shared with you includes a button in the corresponding apps with the name of the person who sent it. You can click the button to continue the conversation about it later, right where you left off.

1. View the content that was shared with you.
   For example, click Shared with You in the News sidebar, then find the article that was shared with you.
2. Click the From button to the right of the content.
3. Compose an inline reply, then press Return on your

   keyboard or click the Send button ⬆ .

Tip: You can hide content that appears in an app's Shared with You section. Control-click the content (or the From button), then choose Remove or Remove Share.

Pin shared content

If you receive content that's especially interesting and you have Shared with You turned on, you can quickly pin it in Messages, and it will be elevated in Shared with You, Messages search, and the Info view of the conversation.

1. In the Messages app ⬤ on your Mac, select a conversation.
2. Control-click the shared content, then choose Pin.
   You can pin content you shared with someone or that someone shared with you.

Tip: You can also find Shared with You content when you search with Spotlight—it's in the Shared Links section.

Play games with your friends

You can play single-player or multiplayer games on your Mac. When you sign in with your Apple ID, a Game Center account is created for you (if it didn't exist already).

You can browse the Mac App Store to get the newest or most popular games that support Game Center. If you're using a Mac with Apple silicon, many iPhone and iPad games work on your Mac (as indicated by the Designed for iPhone or Designed for iPad label in the App Store).

You can also subscribe to Apple Arcade to download and play a collection of groundbreaking games, and enjoy unlimited play on all your supported devices.

Note: The Game Center service and Apple Arcade aren't available in all countries or regions.

Customize your Game Center account

1. On your Mac, choose Apple menu > System Settings, then click Game Center in the sidebar. (You may need to scroll down.)
2. Do any of the following:
   - *Change your nickname:* Enter a new nickname (it identifies you in games), then press Return.
   - *Change who can view your profile:* Click the pop-up menu next to Profile Privacy, then choose who can view your profile in games (Everyone, Friends Only, or Only You). Your profile shows which games you've been playing and your achievements. Your Game Center nickname and avatar are always visible to all players.
   - *Allow friends to find you:* Turn on Allow Finding by Friends so your friends can find you based on the name they have for you in their contacts list in the Contacts app.
   - *Allow requests from contacts only:* Turn on Requests from Contacts Only so the only friend requests you receive are from your contacts.
   - *Allow nearby players to invite you to a multiplayer game:* Turn on Nearby Players. If you don't want to be found, turn it off. Nearby players are those on the same Wi-Fi network as you, or within Bluetooth® range.
   - *Connect with friends:* Turn on Connect with Friends to allow games you play to connect to people in your friends list. If you don't want games to connect to your friends, turn it off to stop sharing your friends list with apps.
   - *Invite friends:* Click Invite Friends to send invitations using the Messages app.
   - *Add or remove friends:* Click Show Profile to open your Game Center profile in the App Store.

When you sign in with your Apple ID on all your Apple devices, your Game Center account is available on all the devices.

Use a game controller

You can connect a game controller with your Mac to play games.

If your game controller supports it, you can specify actions to occur on your Mac—for example, open the Games folder in Launchpad, take a screenshot, or record a brief video of gameplay—when you press designated buttons on the game controller. To set these options when your game controller is connected to your Mac, choose Apple menu > System Settings, then click Game Controller in the sidebar. (You may need to scroll down.)

Open a game

Games you download from the App Store are added to the Games folder in Launchpad. To open a game and start playing on your Mac, do one of the following:

- Click the Launchpad icon in the Dock, click the Games folder, then open the game you want to play.
- If you're using a Bluetooth game controller that supports it, press the designated button on the game controller to open the Games folder, then open the game you want to play.

If you don't play a game anymore, you can easily remove it from Launchpad.

See your achievements

Most single-player and multiplayer games show achievements and leaderboards so you can track your scores and ranking. You can access your Game Center Profile to track your achievements and show which games your friends are playing.

Play multiplayer games

Note: Compatible hardware and software are required to play some games.

- *Let a game find other players:* If the game provides Auto-match, click Play Now to let the game find other players for you.

193

- *Play nearby players:* If the game detects nearby players who are on the same Wi-Fi network as you, or within Bluetooth range, it shows them. In the game, select a player.
- *Invite friends to play:* In the game, click Invite Friends, then select people from your contacts, friends, or nearby players. Customize your invitation, if you want, then click Send. You can send your invitation as a message, or send it to a phone number using SMS.
- *Accept an invitation:* In the notification or message, click Accept. The game opens (if you have it) so you can start playing. If you don't have the game, the App Store opens so you can get the game.
- *Record a brief video or take a screenshot while playing:* When you use a Bluetooth game controller that supports it, press and hold the game controller button you specified to use for recording or taking a screenshot. You can record up to 15 seconds of gameplay.

Make sure Game Center notifications are turned on in Notifications settings, so you know when you're invited to join a game or that it's your turn to play. You can receive Game Center notifications even when you're using a Focus.

When you play games on a Mac connected to a display that supports adaptive sync, you can set an option that automatically adjusts the display's refresh rate to match the frame rate output by the graphics processing unit (GPU), to minimize screen stutters, input lag, and screen tearing during gameplay.

The administrator of a Mac can prevent other users of the Mac from joining multiplayer games or adding friends.

Listen, watch, and read

Play music

Listen to your music the way you like—use the controls in the Music window to repeat songs, change the order they play in, and more.
Siri: Say something like:

- "Play some music"
- "Play the DATA album"
- "What song is this?"
- "Pause music playback"
- "Resume music playback"

1. In the Music app 🎵 on your Mac, do any of the following to find music in your music library:
   - Find a specific song or album: Click any item below Library in the sidebar. For example, click Albums to display all the albums in your library.
   - Choose a playlist: Select a playlist below Playlists in the sidebar.
   - Search your music library
2. Move the pointer over any song or album, then click the Play button ▶.

Listen to podcasts

When you find a podcast you want to listen to, you can play the show or specific episodes of the show. You can also follow a show so that new episodes are automatically downloaded to your library as they become available.

1. In the Podcasts app 🎙 on your Mac, click any item in the sidebar.
2. Hold the pointer over the show or episode you want to play, then click the Play button ▶.
   When the episode plays, the playback controls and show art appear at the top of the Podcasts window. Some shows feature unique artwork for each episode, which appears in

the player and on the episode page.

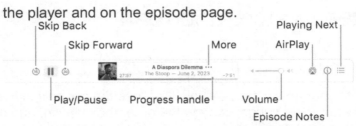

Skip Back

Skip Forward   More   AirPlay

Playing Next

Play/Pause   Progress handle   Volume

Episode Notes

3. Do any of the following with the playback controls:

- *Play or pause:* Click the center Play button ▶ or Pause button ❚❚ (or use the playback controls in the Touch Bar).
  You can also press the Space bar to play, pause, and resume playing an episode.

- *Skip backward or forward:* Click the Skip Back button ⟲15 to go back (in 15-second increments) and the Skip Forward button ⟳30 to skip ahead (in 30-second increments) in the episode (or use the playback controls in the Touch Bar).
  Tip: You can customize the amount of time an episode goes back or skips ahead.

- *Rewind or fast-forward:* Click a point on the progress bar to skip directly to that location, or drag the progress handle left to rewind or right to fast-forward. (You can also use the playback controls in the Touch Bar.)

- *Change the playback speed:* Choose Controls > Playback Speed, then choose a speed.

- *Adjust volume:* Drag the volume slider right or left to increase or decrease the volume (or use the playback controls in the Touch Bar).

- *Choose speakers:* Click the AirPlay button 🔊 to choose which speakers you want to use.

- *Manage the episode (for example, copy the link, share the episode, or go to the Show page):* Hold the pointer over the episode playing, click the More button ⋯, then choose an option.

196

- Read the episode description: Click the Episode Notes button (i). The episode description appears onscreen until you click (i) again to close it.

Siri: Say something like:

- "Skip ahead 3 minutes"
- "Continue playing the last podcast"

Some shows or episodes may require a subscription to access content.

Your podcasts information—episodes you saved, shows you follow, your channel subscriptions, your stations, and current play position—syncs to the Podcasts app on all your devices when you sign in with the same Apple ID.

To learn more about how Podcasts protects your information and lets you choose what you share, choose Help > About Apple Podcasts & Privacy.

Watch TV shows and movies

Watch Now in the Apple TV app is the place to start watching movies, TV shows, and Friday Night Baseball (not all content is available in all countries or regions). In Watch Now, you can also find Major League Soccer matches when you subscribe to MLS Season Pass. Find what you want to watch, add it to your Up Next list, then start watching.

Browse content

1. Open the Apple TV app on your Mac.
2. Click Watch Now in the sidebar.
   The Up Next row displays content you've added to Up Next, as well as content you've started watching but haven't finished.
3. Scroll down to view recommended TV shows, movies, and events—including collections hand-picked by experts,

categories based on your viewing history, and friends' suggestions shared with you from the Messages app.
4. Click an item to see its rating, description, available viewing options, and purchase or rental information.

Play a movie, TV show, or sports event

1. In the Apple TV app [apple tv icon] on your Mac, click an item in the Watch Now window.
2. Do any of the following:
    - *Play the item:* Click Play. (The Play button is available for free content, content you've already purchased, or content on Apple TV channels you subscribe to.)
    - *Subscribe to Apple TV+:* Click the subscription button, then follow the onscreen instructions.
    - *Subscribe to an Apple TV channel:* Click the subscription button, then follow the onscreen instructions.
    - *Buy or rent a movie or TV show:* Click Buy or Rent, then select the option you want and confirm your purchase or rental.
    - *Watch a sports event marked live:* Click Watch to go directly to the event, or click the Add button [+ icon] in the upper-right corner to add it to the Up Next row for watching later.

Listen to live local radio during MLS matches or Friday Night Baseball

1. While playing an MLS match or Friday Night Baseball game in the Apple TV app [apple tv icon] on your Mac, move the pointer over the viewing area to show playback controls.
2. Select the Audio Options button [audio icon] in the lower-right corner, then choose an audio track option from the pop-up menu:
    - *TV:* Play the audio commentary from the TV broadcast.

- Away Team's Local Radio: Listen to the away team's local radio broadcast while watching the game (this option is only available for Friday Night Baseball games).
- Home Team's Local Radio: Listen to the home team's radio broadcast while watching the match or game.

See what's up next

The Up Next row displays content you've already started to watch or plan to watch.

- In the Watch Now window of the Apple TV app tv on your Mac, scroll to the Up Next row to see shows you've recently watched or added to Up Next. To see additional items, move the pointer to the beginning or end of the row, then click the arrow that appears.
Shows and movies appear in the order you're most likely to want to watch them. For example, when a TV episode is finished, the next episode automatically appears in Up Next. And if you've already caught up on a show, whenever a new episode becomes available, it immediately appears in the beginning of the Up Next row.
If you have an iPhone, iPad, iPod touch, or Apple TV and are signed in with the same Apple ID you use for the Mac, your viewing progress and episode selection stay in sync in the Apple TV app on those devices. For example, you can start watching a show on your Mac and finish watching it on your iPad, or vice versa.

Add a movie, TV show, or sports event to Up Next

In the Watch Now window of the Apple TV app tv on your Mac, do either of the following:

- Move the pointer over a movie, show, or event thumbnail, click the More button ••• that appears, then choose Add to Up Next.

- Click a movie, show, or event thumbnail, then click the Add button ⊞ in the upper-right corner.

Remove an item from Up Next

- In the Watch Now window of the Apple TV app on your Mac, move the pointer over an item in the Up Next row, click the More button that appears, then choose Remove from Up Next.

Share an item from Up Next

1. In the Watch Now window of the Apple TV app on your Mac, move the pointer over an item in the Up Next row, then click the More button that appears.
2. Choose Share Show or Share Movie, then choose a sharing option.

Start watching from Up Next

- In the Watch Now window of the Apple TV app on your Mac, move the pointer over a thumbnail in the Up Next row, then click the Play button that appears.

Read and listen to books

After you get books from the Book Store or download books you purchased on other devices, you can start reading and enjoying them.

If you'd rather have a book read to you, you might enjoy listening to audiobooks.

See the Table of Contents.

See your bookmarks.

Bookmark a page.

Two o'clock struck. This was becoming ridiculous; worse than that, unbearable. I began to say to myself that I was exaggerating the importance of the document; that my uncle would surely not believe in it, that he would set it down as a mere puzzle; that if it came to the worst, we should lay violent hands on him and keep him at home if he thought on venturing on the expedition that, after all, he might himself discover the key of the cipher, and that then I should be clear at the mere expense of my involuntary abstinence.

These reasons seemed excellent to me, though on the night before I should have rejected them with indignation; I even went so far as to condemn myself for my absurdity in having waited so long, and I finally resolved to let it all out.

I was therefore meditating a proper introduction to the matter, so as not to seem too abrupt, when the Professor jumped up, clapped on his hat, and prepared to go out.

Surely he was not going out, to shut us in again! no, never!

"Uncle!" I cried.

He seemed not to hear me.

"Uncle Liedenbrock!" I cried, lifting up my voice.

"Ay," he answered like a man suddenly waking.

"Uncle, that key!"

"What key? The door key?"

"No, no!" I cried. "The key of the document."

The Professor stared at me over his spectacles; no doubt he saw something unusual in the expression of my countenance; for he laid hold of my arm, and speechlessly questioned me with his eyes. Yes, never was a question more forcibly put.

I nodded my head up and down.

He shook his pityingly, as if he was dealing with a lunatic. I gave a more affirmative gesture.

His eyes glistened and sparkled with live fire, his hand was shaken threateningly.

This mute conversation at such a momentous crisis would have riveted the attention of the most indifferent. And the fact really was that I dared not speak now, so intense was the excitement for fear lest my uncle should smother me in his first joyful embraces.

Open and move around in a book

1. In the Books app on your Mac, click Books (or another collection) in the sidebar, then double-click a book to open it.

   Note: If the book has an iCloud status icon ☁ underneath it, you can double-click the book to download it from iCloud (you might need to sign in first).

2. Move around the book:

   o *See the table of contents:* Move the pointer to the top of the book, then click the Table of Contents button ☷ or the Thumbnails button ⊟, depending on the book.

   o *Go to the next or previous page:* Move the pointer to the right or left edge of the book, then click the arrow that appears.
   You can also swipe right or left across a trackpad or Magic Mouse, use the Touch Bar, or use the arrow keys on the keyboard.

   o *Search in the book:* Move the pointer to the top of the book, click the magnifying glass 🔍, then enter a word, phrase, or page number. You can also select text, Control-click it, then choose Search.

- ○ *See the last page you viewed:* Click the Go Back icon

  ⟳ at the lower-left corner of the page. This is useful if you're viewing search results or different sections in the book's table of contents.

  To return to the page you started on, click the Return icon ⟳ in the lower-right corner of the page.

See what you're currently reading

- In the Books app 📖 on your Mac, click Reading Now in the sidebar.

  To remove a book or audiobook from Reading Now, move the pointer below the title, click the More button •••, click Remove, then click Remove from Collection.

Save your place with a bookmark

1. In the Books app 📖 on your Mac, click Books (or another collection) in the sidebar, then double-click a book to open it.
2. On the page you want to bookmark, move the pointer to the top of the page, then click the Bookmark button 🔖 (or use the Touch Bar).

   If the page is already bookmarked, the Bookmark button is solid.

To see all the bookmarks in a book, click the Show Bookmarks button 🔖. If you want to remove a bookmark, click the Bookmark button 🔖.

Have a book read to you

1. In the Books app 📖 on your Mac, click Books (or another collection) in the sidebar, then double-click a book to open it.
2. Do one of the following:

- For books that include the Read Aloud feature: Click the Play button ▶ in the toolbar at the top of the book (or use the Touch Bar). Click the pop-up menu next to the Play button, then choose a page turning option.
- For any book: Go to the page you want, then choose Edit > Speech > Start Speaking.

Read information about a book or audiobook

You can view descriptions and details for content that you purchased from the Book Store or Audiobook Store.

1. In the Books app 📖 on your Mac, click any collection below Library in the sidebar.
2. Click the More button ••• for the item, then click View in Store.

Translate text in a book

1. In the Books app 📖 on your Mac, select the text you want to translate.
2. Control-click the selection, then choose Translate [selection]. (If you don't see this option, you can't translate this text in Books.)
3. Choose the current language, then choose which language you want to translate to.

Delay when the display sleeps while reading

1. In the Books app 📖 on your Mac, choose Books > Settings, then click Reading.
2. Select or deselect "Extend by 10 minutes while reading."

Read the news

Apple News collects and organizes stories from a wide range of publications (called channels) and topics. It's easy to explore what's there and find the sources and stories that interest you—from breaking news to travel videos to summer recipes.

Note: Apple News and Apple News+ aren't available in all countries or regions.

1. In the News app on your Mac, click an item in the sidebar.

   If the sidebar isn't shown, click in the toolbar.
   In addition to quick access to stories you saved and your reading history, the sidebar includes the following:
   - *Today*, which presents top stories selected by Apple News editors and stories from the channels and topics you follow. In some countries or regions, the Today feed can include local news, featuring curated and personalized local stories and weather reports based on your location.
     If you subscribe to Apple News+, the Today feed also includes My Magazines, which shows issues from magazines you follow.
   - *News+*, which presents hundreds of magazines, popular newspapers, and other publications available from Apple News+. If you're a subscriber, you can browse recent issues, download issues, click a publication to read it, and more. If you don't subscribe yet, you can browse publications and headlines.
   - *Sports*, where you can follow your favorite sports, leagues, teams, and athletes; receive stories from top sports publications, local newspapers, and more; access scores, schedules, and standings for the top professional and college leagues; and watch highlights.
   - *Puzzles*, where Apple News+ subscribers can solve daily crossword and crossword mini puzzles.
   - *Shared with You*, which shows stories that others have shared with you using the Messages app, so it's easy to find and read them in one location.
   - *Favorites*, which shows the channels and topics from your Following list that you like best (you can have only a limited number of Favorites). You may already have some channels and topics that have been

automatically added to Favorites, but you can customize this list at any time.

- *Following*, which lists the channels and topics you follow. This section also includes Apple News Spotlight, which showcases coverage of special events and content selected by Apple News editors.
- *Suggested*, which lists channels and topics suggested by Siri or—if you chose not to have Siri suggest items—by your actions in Apple News. For example, whether you follow or block channels and topics, or ask for more or fewer suggestions similar to a story you're reading. In some countries or regions, local news may be suggested based on your location.

2. If a channel or topic you expected isn't shown, use the search field at the top of the sidebar to search Apple News, or choose File > Discover Channels.
3. On the right, browse stories or the News+ Library.
When you browse Top Stories and other areas that feature stories curated by Apple News editors, stories from channels you blocked show a gray headline and a message indicating that you blocked the channel.
4. Click a story to read it or, in the News+ Library, click a publication to explore issues and stories.
As you read a story, you can do any of the following:
   - Watch videos, ask to show more or fewer stories like it, share it with others, or save it to read later.
   - Move to the next or previous story by pressing the Right Arrow or Left Arrow key.
   - Go directly to the story's channel—just click the Share button in the toolbar, then choose Go to Channel.

You can set an option in News settings for the Today and other feeds to show only stories from the channels you follow.

Tip: You can stop some channels and topics—such as Travel or Food—from being suggested in the Today feed. Next to the item in the feed, click the More button , then choose Stop Suggesting. If you change your mind and want Apple News to suggest the channel or topic again, search for it, then follow it.

Track stocks and the market

Customize your watchlists to display the ticker symbols you view regularly.

When you add a ticker symbol to a watchlist you created, it's also added to the My Symbols watchlist. The My Symbols watchlist contains your complete library of ticker symbols; the watchlists you create contain just the ticker symbols you add to them.

You don't need to know a specific ticker symbol to add it to your list. Just knowing the name is enough to get you started.

Type a name or ticker symbol in the search field.

Click to add the selected ticker symbol to your watchlist.

Find and add new ticker symbols

Search for the ticker symbols you want to follow and add them to your watchlists.

1. In the Stocks app on your Mac, click the name of the current watchlist at the top of the sidebar, then choose a watchlist.
2. Type a name or ticker symbol in the search field.
3. Do one of the following:
   - Click the Add button ➕ next to the ticker symbol in the sidebar to add it to the current watchlist and the My Symbols watchlist.
   - Click the ticker symbol in the sidebar, then click the Add to Watchlist button ➕∨ in the toolbar to add it

206

to the current watchlist, the My Symbols watchlist, and any additional watchlists you select.

To clear the search field and return to your watchlist, click the Delete button ⊗ in the search field.

Tip: Each entry in the search results list shows the exchange the ticker symbol trades on and the currency code. Many securities trade on multiple exchanges—use that information to help choose the right ticker symbol to add to your watchlists.

Add ticker symbols to another watchlist

1. In the Stocks app 📈 on your Mac, click the ticker symbol you want to add to another watchlist.
2. Do one of the following:
   - Click the Manage Symbol button ✓˅ in the toolbar.
   - Swipe left, then click the Add to Watchlist button ☰.
3. Select the checkbox next to each watchlist you want the ticker symbol to appear in.

Remove ticker symbols from watchlists

When you remove a symbol from the My Symbols watchlist, it's removed from every watchlist that contains it. When you remove a symbol from a watchlist you created, it's removed from only that watchlist—it remains in the My Symbols watchlist.

1. In the Stocks app 📈 on your Mac, click the name of the current watchlist at the top of the sidebar, then do one of the following:
   - Choose the My Symbols watchlist to remove a ticker symbol from all watchlists it appears in, including the My Symbols watchlist and any watchlists you created.
   - Choose a watchlist you created to remove a ticker symbol from just that watchlist.
2. Click the ticker symbol you want to remove.

3. Do one of the following:
   - ○ Swipe left, then click the Trash button 🗑.
   - ○ Press the Delete key, then click Remove.
   - ○ Click the Manage Symbol button ✓ˇ in the toolbar, then deselect the checkbox next to each watchlist you want to remove the symbol from.

Reorder ticker symbols in a watchlist

1. In the Stocks app 📈 on your Mac, click the name of the current watchlist at the top of the sidebar, then choose the watchlist with ticker symbols you want to reorder.
2. Drag ticker symbols to reorder them.

Sort ticker symbols in a watchlist

Choose how the ticker symbols in each of your watchlists are sorted.

1. In the Stocks app 📈 on your Mac, click the name of the current watchlist at the top of the sidebar, then choose the watchlist with ticker symbols you want to sort.
2. Choose View > Sort Watchlist By, then choose one of the following options:
   - ○ Manual
   - ○ Price Change
   - ○ Percentage Change
   - ○ Market Cap
   - ○ Symbol
   - ○ Name
3. To change the order of the ticker symbols in the watchlist, choose View > Sort Watchlist By, then choose Ascending or Descending.

Manage a ticker symbol

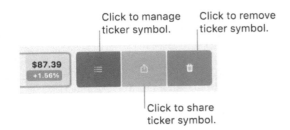

Click to manage ticker symbol.

Click to remove ticker symbol.

$87.39
+1.56%

Click to share ticker symbol.

1. In the Stocks app ![icon] on your Mac, move the pointer over a ticker symbol in a watchlist, then swipe left.

2. Do any of the following:
   - *Add the ticker symbol to watchlists:* Click the Add to Watchlist button ⋮☰, then select the checkbox next to each watchlist you want the ticker symbol to appear in.

   - *Share the ticker symbol:* Click the Share button ⬆, then click a sharing method. For example, choose Notes or Reminders to save a link to the ticker symbol that you can later use to quickly view details about the ticker symbol in the Stocks app.

   - *Remove the ticker symbol:* Click the Trash button 🗑.

Subscribe to services

Apple Music

Apple Music is an ad-free streaming music service that lets you listen to millions of songs from the Apple Music catalog in addition to your music library. As a subscriber, you can listen any time—online or off—create your own playlists, stream and download lossless and Dolby Atmos audio files, get personalized recommendations, see music your friends are listening to, watch exclusive video content, and more.

You can subscribe to Apple Music or to Apple One, which includes Apple Music and other Apple services.

Alternatively, you can subscribe to Apple Music Voice and use Siri to stream any song, album, playlist, or radio station in the Apple Music catalog.

Note: Apple Music, Apple Music Voice, and Apple One aren't available in all countries or regions.

Subscribe to Apple Music

1. In the Music app on your Mac, choose Account > Join Apple Music.
2. Follow the onscreen instructions.
   You may be asked to sign in with your Apple ID. If you don't have an Apple ID, you can create one during setup.

About your Apple Music subscription

After you become an Apple Music subscriber, you can:

- Stream recommended songs on up to 10 computers and devices
- Select artists as favorites to receive notifications about them and easily find their music
- Download songs so that you can listen to them even when you're not online

- Access your music library on all your devices
- Play Apple Music radio—stations created by experts that you can listen to all day
- Listen to music together using SharePlay on a FaceTime call
- Listen to and download songs in lossless audio and Dolby Atmos (spatial) audio
- Create an Apple Music profile and then share music with friends; you can also find and follow friends to see what they're listening to
- Allow third-party apps to access Apple Music, such as a third-party speaker app
- View song lyrics
- Use Autoplay to automatically add similar songs to the end of the queue

Even if you don't subscribe to Apple Music, you can purchase items from the iTunes Store and add music to your library.

Cancel or change your Apple Music subscription

1. In the Music app ♫ on your Mac, choose Account > Account Settings, then sign in.
   You may be asked to sign in with your Apple ID.
2. In the Settings section, click Manage next to Subscriptions.
3. Click Edit next to Apple Music, Apple Music Voice, or Apple One, then do one of the following:
   - *Cancel:* Click Cancel Subscription, then follow the onscreen instructions.
   - *Change:* Choose another plan or click Choose Individual Services, then follow the onscreen instructions.

To learn more about how Apple Music protects your information and lets you choose what you share, choose Help > About Apple Music & Privacy.

Apple TV+

You can subscribe to channels available in the Apple TV app, including Apple TV+ and MLS Season Pass.

Apple TV+ is a subscription streaming service featuring Apple Originals—award-winning films, series, compelling dramas, groundbreaking documentaries, kids' entertainment, comedies, and more—with new items added every month.

MLS Season Pass is a subscription streaming service featuring every match of the Major League Soccer season, all in one place, with consistent match times, and no blackouts.

You can choose to bundle your Apple TV+ subscription with other Apple services by subscribing to Apple One.

Apple TV channels let you easily subscribe to just the channels you watch—like STARZ, Paramount+, and more.

Note: Apple TV+, MLS Season Pass, Apple TV channels, and Apple One aren't available in all countries or regions.

Subscribe to Apple TV+

1. Open the Apple TV app on your Mac.
2. Click Watch Now in the sidebar.
3. In the main window, scroll down to the Channels row, then click Apple TV+.
4. Click the subscription button, then follow the onscreen instructions.
   If you already have an Apple ID, you can sign in to start your free trial.

Subscribe to MLS Season Pass

1. Open the Apple TV app on your Mac.
2. Click MLS in the sidebar.
3. Click the subscription button, then follow the onscreen instructions.

Subscribe to Apple TV channels

1. Open the Apple TV app on your Mac.
2. Click Watch Now in the sidebar.

3. In the main window, scroll down to the Channels row, then click an item.
4. Click the subscription button, then follow the onscreen instructions.

Cancel a subscription

1. In the Apple TV app on your Mac, choose Account > Account Settings.
   You may be asked to sign in with your Apple ID.
2. In the Account Information window, scroll down to the Settings section.
3. Click Manage next to Subscriptions, then follow the onscreen instructions to change or cancel your subscriptions.
4. When you're finished, scroll down and click Done, then scroll down in the Account Information window and click Done.

Share Apple TV+, MLS Season Pass, or Apple TV channels

When you subscribe to Apple TV+, MLS Season Pass, Apple TV channels, or Apple One, you can use Family Sharing to share your subscription with up to five other family members. Your family group members don't need to do anything—Apple TV+ and Apple TV channels are available to them the first time they open the TV app after your subscription begins.

If you join a family group that subscribes to Apple TV+, MLS Season Pass, or Apple One, and you already subscribe, your subscription isn't renewed on your next billing date; instead, you use the group's subscription. If you join a family group that doesn't subscribe, the group uses your subscription.

Note: To stop sharing your Apple TV+ subscription with a family group, you can cancel the subscription, leave the family group, or (if you're the family group organizer) stop using Family Sharing.

Apple Arcade

With a subscription to Apple Arcade, you can download and play a collection of groundbreaking new games from the App Store—on all your supported devices.

You can subscribe to Apple Arcade or to Apple One, which includes Apple Arcade and other services.

Note: Apple Arcade and Apple One aren't available in all countries or regions.. The availability of Apple Arcade games across devices varies based on hardware and software compatibility. Some content may not be available in all areas.

Subscribe to Apple Arcade

1. In the App Store ⚄ on your Mac, click Arcade in the sidebar.
2. Click the subscription button, then follow the onscreen instructions.

Cancel or change your Apple Arcade subscription

1. In the App Store ⚄ on your Mac, click your name in the bottom-left corner, or click Sign In if you're not already.
2. Click Account Settings.
3. In the Manage section, click Manage next to Subscriptions, then click Edit for Apple Arcade or Apple One.
4. Follow the onscreen instructions.
    You can cancel your subscription at any time at least one day before the renewal date.

Share Apple Arcade

When you subscribe to Apple Arcade or Apple One, you can use Family Sharing to share Apple Arcade with up to five other family members. Your family group members don't need to do anything—Apple Arcade is available to them the first time they open it after your subscription begins.

If you join a Family Sharing group that subscribes to Apple Arcade or Apple One, and you already subscribe, your subscription isn't renewed on your next billing date; instead, you use the group's subscription. If you join a family group that doesn't subscribe, the group uses your subscription.

Note: To stop sharing Apple Arcade with a family group, you can cancel the subscription, leave the Family Sharing group, or (if you're the family group organizer) stop using Family Sharing.

Apple News+

Apple News+ lets you enjoy hundreds of magazines, popular newspapers, and content from premium digital publishers directly in Apple News on your Mac.

You can subscribe to Apple News+ or to Apple One Premier, which includes Apple News+ and other Apple services.

Note: Apple News, Apple News+, and Apple One aren't available in all countries or regions.

Subscribe to Apple News+

1. In the News app on your Mac, click News+ in the sidebar (if the sidebar isn't shown, click in the toolbar), then click the subscription button.
2. Follow the onscreen instructions.
    You may be asked to sign in to the App Store with your Apple ID.

Cancel or change your Apple News+ subscription

1. In the News app on your Mac, choose File > Manage Subscriptions.
    You may be asked to sign in to the App Store with your Apple ID.
2. In the Manage section, click Manage next to Subscriptions, then click Edit for Apple News+ or Apple One.
3. Follow the onscreen instructions.

Apple News+ stories you saved and issues you downloaded remain on your Mac unless it requires more disk space, you choose Clear All when you clear your reading history, or you delete issues.

Share Apple News+

When you subscribe to Apple News+ or Apple One Premier, you can use Family Sharing to share Apple News+ with up to five other family members. Your family group members don't need to do anything—Apple News+ is available to them the first time they open the News app after your subscription begins.

If you join a Family Sharing group that subscribes to Apple News+ or Apple One Premier, and you already subscribe, your subscription isn't renewed on your next billing date; instead, you use the group's subscription. If you join a family group that doesn't subscribe, the group uses your subscription.

Note: To stop sharing Apple News+ with a family group, you can cancel the subscription, leave the Family Sharing group, or (if you're the family organizer) stop using Family Sharing.

Podcast shows and channels

A channel is a collection of shows offered by a podcast creator.

You can listen to free shows and channels and purchase a subscription to others for exclusive or early access to subscriber-only audio, ad-free listening, and more.

Note: Subscriptions aren't available in every country or region.

Subscribe to a show or channel

1. In the Podcasts app on your Mac, select the show or channel that you want to subscribe to.
   When you subscribe to a show, you automatically follow it.
2. Click the subscription button.
   If you're using Family Sharing and someone in your family group subscribes to a show or channel, Podcasts shows a message that you already have access.

You may be asked to enter your Apple ID and password. Make sure you sign in with the same Apple ID you use for App Store and iTunes Store purchases.

3. Choose a subscription option that's available from the podcast creator (for example, annual or monthly).

When you subscribe to a channel, you can quickly access it by clicking Channels in the sidebar.

Connect app subscriptions to Podcasts

Your eligible app subscriptions are automatically connected to Podcasts if you subscribed through the App Store and the app offers audio content in Podcasts.

If you subscribed using another method, do the following:

1. Open the Podcasts app on your Mac, then browse or search for a channel with an eligible subscription.
2. On the Channel page, tap the Already a Subscriber link, then follow the instructions to connect your app subscription.

Cancel or change your subscription

You can view or change subscriptions you purchased in the Podcasts app, the App Store, the Apple TV app, the iTunes Store, or Apple News.

1. In the Podcasts app on your Mac, choose Account > View Apple ID. Media & Purchases settings opens.
2. Click Manage next to Subscriptions.
3. Click Edit next to a subscription, then do any of the following:
   - *Change subscription options:* In the Options list, select a setting, then click Done.
   - *Cancel your subscription:* Click Cancel Subscription, confirm the cancellation, then click Done.

Share Apple Podcasts subscriptions

When you subscribe to shows or channels, you can use Family Sharing to share your subscriptions with up to five other family members. Your family group members automatically have access to the shows and channels you subscribe to.

If you join a family group and a family group member subscribes to a show or channel you already subscribe to, your subscription isn't renewed on your next billing date; instead, you use the group's subscription. If you join a family group that doesn't subscribe, the group uses your subscription.

Note: To stop sharing an Apple Podcasts subscription with a family group, you can cancel the subscription, leave the family group, or (if you're the family group organizer) stop using Family Sharing.

To learn more about how Podcasts protects your information and lets you choose what you share, choose Help > About Apple Podcasts & Privacy.

Manage subscriptions in the App Store

You can view or change options for your Apple One subscription or other subscriptions you purchased in the App Store, the Apple TV app, the iTunes Store, or Apple News. You can also share eligible App Store subscriptions with family members.

Cancel or change a subscription

1. In the App Store on your Mac, click your name in the bottom-left corner, or click Sign In if you're not already. Make sure you sign in with the same Apple ID you used to

purchase your subscriptions.

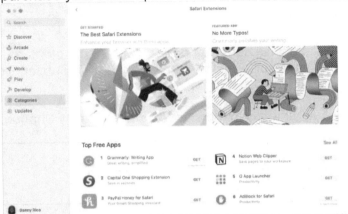

2. Click Account Settings, sign in again if necessary, then click Manage (in the Manage section, to the right of Subscriptions).
3. Click Edit (if you have more than one subscription), then do any of the following:
   ○ *Cancel a subscription:* Click Cancel Subscription, confirm the cancellation, then click Done.
   ○ *Change a subscription:* In the Options list, select a setting, then click Done.

Share subscriptions with family

1. In the App Store on your Mac, click your name in the bottom-left corner, or click Sign In if you're not already. Make sure you sign in with the same Apple ID you used to purchase your subscriptions.
2. Click Account Settings, sign in again if necessary, then click Manage (in the Manage section, to the right of Subscriptions).
3. Choose Share New Subscriptions.
   Sharing subscriptions requires one adult in your household—the family organizer—to set up Family Sharing.

View Apple family subscriptions

On your Mac, you can subscribe to Apple Music, Apple TV+, Apple Arcade, Apple News+, and more, and share your subscriptions with family members. Use Subscriptions settings in Family Sharing to see the services you can share with family members.

To view the available subscriptions, choose Apple menu > System Settings, click Family in the sidebar, click Subscriptions on the right, then click Apple Subscriptions.

If you don't see Family in the sidebar, set up Family Sharing.

Option	Description
Apple Subscriptions for Your Family	Click the Learn More button next to a service to find out more about it or to manage your existing subscriptions. You can subscribe to Apple services and share them with family members. For example, you can create an Apple Music Family Plan membership and share over 90 million songs with your Family Sharing group. The subscriptions in the list change as new services become available.

Privacy and security

Guard your privacy

Privacy is an important concern when using apps that exchange information across the internet. macOS includes security features to enhance your privacy and control the amount of information that's exposed about you and your Mac over the internet.

Use Screen Time

You can use Screen Time to monitor your children's computer use and limit their access to websites.

Choose Apple menu > System Settings, then click Screen Time in the sidebar. (You may need to scroll down.)

Use the privacy features in Safari

Safari provides numerous features to help you control your privacy on the internet. You can browse privately, so Safari doesn't keep a record of websites you visited or items you downloaded. You can view a Privacy Report to see who was blocked from tracking you. You can allow or block pop-up windows, clear cookies on your Mac, and more.

Control the personal information you share with apps

Location Services lets apps, such as web browsers, gather and use information based on your location. You can turn off Location Services completely, or you can select which apps can see information about your location.

Some apps may gather and use information from your contacts, photos, calendar, or reminders. Some apps may access the microphone or camera on your Mac.

Choose whether to share analytics information

You can help Apple improve the quality and performance of its products and services. macOS can automatically collect analytics information from your Mac and send it to Apple for analysis. The information is sent only with your consent and is submitted anonymously to Apple.

To choose whether analytics data is sent to Apple, use Privacy & Security settings.

Choose Apple menu > System Settings, click Privacy & Security in the sidebar, then click Analytics & Improvements on the right. (You may need to scroll down.)

Set up a firewall

You can use a firewall to protect your privacy by blocking unwanted network communications with your Mac. If the firewall is on, you can also use "stealth mode," which prevents your Mac from being discovered by others on the web.

To set up and customize your firewall, use Network settings.

Choose Apple menu > System Settings, click Network in the sidebar, then click Firewall on the right. (You may need to scroll down.)

Use Mail Privacy Protection

The Mail app can help protect your privacy. Email messages you receive may include remote content that allows a sender to collect information when you view a message, such as when and how many times you view it, whether you forward it, your IP address, and other data. Mail Privacy Protection prevents senders from learning your information.

If you didn't turn on Protect Mail Activity when you first opened Mail in macOS Ventura, you can do so in Mail settings.

1. In the Mail app 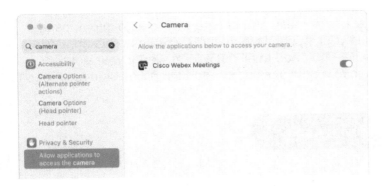 on your Mac, choose Mail > Settings, then click Privacy.
2. Select Protect Mail Activity.
   When this option is selected, your IP address is hidden from senders and remote content is privately downloaded in the background when you receive a message (instead of when you view it).
   If you deselect the option, you can choose to separately hide your IP address and block all remote content. When Block All Remote Content is selected, a banner is shown in a message when you view it, indicating it contains remote content; you can choose then to download the content.

Note: If you turned off the option in Network settings to limit IP address tracking for your Wi-Fi or Ethernet network, your IP address isn't hidden from senders when using the network.

Control access to your camera

Some apps you install can use the camera on your Mac to take photos and video. You can decide which apps are allowed to use the camera.

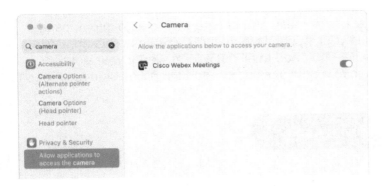

1. Choose Apple menu > System Settings, then click Privacy & Security in the sidebar. (You may need to scroll down.)
2. Click Camera on the right.
   If you don't see Camera, upgrade to macOS Mojave or later.

3. Turn access to the camera on or off for each app in the list.
   The list shows apps you've installed that have asked to use the camera. If you turn off access for an app, you're asked to turn it on again the next time that app tries to use the camera.
   If there are no apps in the list, you haven't installed an app that uses the camera. FaceTime, Photo Booth, and other apps that come with your Mac automatically have access—you don't need to give them permission.
   Note: The camera automatically turns on when you open an app that can use the camera. A green light beside the camera glows to indicate the camera is on. The camera (and the green light) turn off when you close or quit all apps that can use the camera.
   In Safari, to allow a website to use the camera, choose Safari > Settings, click Websites, then select Camera.

If you allow third-party apps or websites to use the camera, any information they collect is governed by their terms and privacy policies. It's recommended that you learn about the privacy practices of those parties.

Use Sign in with Apple for apps and websites

Sign in with Apple is an easy and private way to sign into apps and websites. It uses your Apple ID to securely create an account with an app or website—no need to fill out a form, verify your email address, or choose a new password—and simplifies signing in each time.

Create an account for an app or website

1. On your Mac, when you're asked to create an account for an app or a website, click the button to sign in or continue with Apple, if available.
2. Follow the onscreen instructions, keeping the following in mind:

224

- If you don't want to use your real name, click the Name field, then enter a different name.
- If you have more than one email address associated with your Apple ID in Apple ID settings, choose which email to use for the app or website.
- If you prefer to keep your email address private, click Hide My Email. Apple generates a random and unique email address that's used to forward emails from the app or website to your real email address.

Sign in to your account for an app or website

1. On your Mac, click the button to sign in or continue with Apple.
2. Enter your login password on your Mac (you may need to enter your Apple ID password instead) or, if your Mac or Magic Keyboard has Touch ID, use Touch ID.

You can also sign in from your other devices—iPhone, iPad, Apple Watch, and Apple TV—where you're signed in with the same Apple ID.

Change Sign in with Apple settings for an app or website

1. On your Mac, choose Apple menu > System Settings, then click [your name] at the top of the sidebar. If you don't see your name, click Sign in with Your Apple ID to enter your Apple ID or to create one.
2. Click Sign-In & Security on the right, then click Edit next to Apps Using Apple ID.
3. Click an app or website in the sidebar, then do any of the following:
   - *Turn off forwarding email:* Turn off Forward To. You won't receive any further emails from the app or website.
   - *Stop using Sign in with Apple:* Click Stop Using Apple ID. You may be asked to create a new account the next time you try to sign in with the app or website.

Change the address used to forward email from apps and websites

If you chose to hide your email when you created an account for an app or website, and you have more than one email address associated with your Apple ID in Apple ID settings, you can change the address that receives forwarded email.

Set up your Mac to be secure

Here are some things you can do to make your Mac more secure.

Use secure passwords

To keep your information safe, you should use passwords to secure your Mac, and choose passwords that can't be easily guessed.

Create passkeys

A passkey is a way to sign in to an app or website account, without needing to create and remember a password. Instead of a password, a passkey uses Touch ID or Face ID to identify you.

Require users to log in

If others can get physical access to your Mac, you should set up separate users for each person using the Mac, and require each user to log in. This prevents an unauthorized person from using the Mac. It also separates user files, so users only have access to their own personal files and settings. Users cannot see or modify the files or settings of other users.

Secure your Mac when it's idle

You can set your Mac to log out the current user if the Mac has been inactive for a certain period of time. You should also require a password to wake it from sleep or from the screen saver. For convenience, you can set up a hot corner to click whenever you want to immediately lock your screen.

Limit the number of administrative users

One or more people can have administrator privileges for a Mac. By default the administrator is the person who initially set up the Mac.

Administrators can create, manage, and delete other users; install and remove software; and change settings. For these reasons, an administrator should create a standard user account to use when administrator privileges are not needed. If the security of a standard user is compromised, the potential harm is far more limited than if the user has administrator privileges. If multiple people use your Mac, limit the number of users with administrator privileges.

Protected the encrypted data on your Mac with FileVault

If you have a Mac with Apple silicon or an Apple T2 Security Chip, your data is encrypted automatically. FileVault provides further protection by requiring your login password to see your data.

Keep your data safe

To protect the information on your Mac, perform regular backups, limit access to your information, install software updates, take precautions to find or deactivate a lost computer, and avoid malware.

Perform regular backups

You should always back up your Mac. That way, if something happens to your Mac or you accidentally delete something, you can easily recover your files.

The easiest way to back up is to set up Time Machine, which backs up all the information on your Mac automatically every day.

Besides Time Machine, you have several other choices for backing up your important files, including burning CDs and DVDs, and copying files onto an external drive.

Limit unwanted access to your information

macOS has a number of features to help keep the information on your Mac safe. If multiple people use your Mac, you should set up a user account for each person, so that one person can't modify the files needed by another.

Use secure passwords to prevent unauthorized access, make sure all user accounts have passwords, and turn off automatic login in Users & Groups settings.

To open Users & Groups settings, choose Apple menu > System Settings, then click Users & Groups in the sidebar. (You may need to scroll down.)

Install software updates promptly

Your Mac is already set up to automatically check for software updates and to alert you when updates are available for you to download. The best way to avoid viruses and other problems is to promptly download and install these updates, which contain the latest security software.

To check for available updates, choose Apple menu > System Settings, click General in the sidebar, then click Software Update on the right. (You may need to scroll down.)

If nothing happens when you check for updates, you may not be connected to the internet.

Locate a lost Mac

You can use the Find My app to locate or deactivate a lost Mac from a web browser or an iPhone, iPad, or iPod touch.

Avoid harmful software

Malicious software, or malware, is a threat to all computer users, especially those connected to the internet.

Create a passkey

A passkey is a way to sign in to an app or website account, without needing to create and remember a password. Instead of a password, a passkey uses Touch ID or Face ID to identify you.

If your Mac or Magic Keyboard has Touch ID, you can sign in with Touch ID. You can also sign in with an iPhone or iPad by scanning a QR code and using Face ID to verify your identity.

Create a passkey for a new account

1. When you sign up for a new account, enter an account name, then click to submit.
   To create a passkey, iCloud Keychain must be set up on your Mac.
2. When you see the option to save a passkey for the account, choose how you want to sign in:
   o *Touch ID on your Mac:* Place your finger on the Touch ID sensor.
   o *Scan a QR code with your iPhone or iPad:* Click Other Options.
   o *External security key:* Click Other Options.

Replace the password for an existing account with a passkey

1. Sign in to the account with your password.
2. Choose Apple menu > System Settings, then click Passwords in the sidebar. (You may need to scroll down.)
3. Click the Info button for the website.
4. Click Change Password on Website.

Sign in to an account with a passkey

1. On the account sign-in page, enter your account name, then click the account name field.
2. Click your account in the list of suggestions.

3. Do one of the following:
    ○ *If you have Touch ID on your Mac:* Place your finger on the Touch ID sensor.
    ○ *If you have an iPhone or iPad:* Click Other Options, click "Passkey from nearby device," then click the QR code.
       Note: Bluetooth® must be turned on in Settings > Bluetooth for your iPhone or iPad. Bluetooth must also be turned on for your Mac.
    ○ *External security key:* Click Other Options, click "Security key," then follow the instructions onscreen.

Each passkey is stored in iCloud Keychain, so they're available on all devices where you're signed in with your Apple ID (iOS 16, iPadOS 16, or macOS 13 required).

Understand passwords

macOS is designed to keep your information safe and secure. The security of your Mac depends a great deal on using secure passwords in key areas.

Login password

A login password, also called a *user password*, allows you to log in and access the information on your Mac. When you create your login password, be sure it's easily memorable, write it down, and keep it in a secure location.

Apple ID password

An Apple ID gives you access to the iTunes Store, the App Store, Apple Books, iCloud, FaceTime, and other Apple services. It consists of an email address (for example, daniel_rico1@icloud.com) and a password. Apple recommends you use the same Apple ID for all Apple services. When you create your Apple ID password, be sure it's easily memorable, write it down, and keep it in a secure location. If you can't remember your Apple ID password, see If you forget your Apple ID password.

You can also use your Apple ID to reset your login password if you forget it. Sign in to your Apple ID account page.

Website passwords

When you need to create a password for a website, Safari suggests a unique, hard-to-guess (or "strong") password. It's recommended that you use the suggested password or create a passkey. Passwords and passkeys are saved in a keychain, then automatically filled the next time you need to sign in.

To view or change passwords and passkeys you've saved for websites, use Passwords settings. Choose Apple menu > System Settings, then click Passwords in the sidebar. (You may need to scroll down.)

Password keychains

A keychain saves your passwords and fills them in automatically when you sign in to websites, apps, and services. You can store passwords in Keychain Access and iCloud Keychain.

- *Keychain Access:* Keychain Access stores passwords for various apps and services for your Mac. Your keychain password (which unlocks your keychain) is set to match the login password for your Mac.
- *iCloud Keychain:* iCloud Keychain keeps your passwords up to date across your Mac, iPhone, iPad, and iPod touch. It stores website and Wi-Fi passwords, and it keeps account passwords and settings that you add to Internet Accounts settings up to date on your Mac.

About your recovery key

If you protect the information on your Mac using FileVault, you can choose how to unlock your disk and reset your login password if you forget it: using your iCloud account or a recovery key. A recovery key is a string of letters and numbers that's created for you. The recovery key should not be stored in the same location as the Mac, where it can be discovered.

Keep your Apple ID secure

Your Apple ID is the account you use to access Apple services like the App Store, Apple Music, iCloud, iMessage, FaceTime, and more. Your account includes the email address and password you use to sign in as well as the contact, payment, and security details you use across Apple services.

Best practices for maximizing the security of your Apple ID

- Don't share your Apple ID with other people, even family members.
  You can name up to five people you trust as Account Recovery Contacts to help you regain access to your account if you ever get locked out. You can also assign a person as a Legacy Contact in the event of your passing. To share purchases, subscriptions, a family calendar, and more without sharing Apple IDs, set up Family Sharing.
- Don't provide your password, security questions, verification codes, recovery key, or any other account security details to anyone else. Apple will never ask you for this information.
- Don't use your Apple ID password with other online accounts.
- When using a public computer, always sign out when your session is complete to prevent other people from accessing your account.
- Let two-factor authentication protect your account. If you create a new Apple ID on a device with iOS 13.4, iPadOS 13.4, macOS 10.15.4, or later, your account automatically uses two-factor authentication. If you previously created an Apple ID account without two-factor authentication, turn on two-factor authentication.

Find a missing device

In the Find My app on your Mac, you can see the location of a missing Apple device or get notified when it's located. To locate a missing device, you must add it to Find My *before* it's lost.

Tip: You can also locate a device online in Find Devices on iCloud.com.

See the location of a device

1. In the Find My app on your Mac, click Devices.
2. In the Devices list, select the device you want to locate.
   - *If the device can be located:* It appears on the map so you can see where it is. The updated location and timestamp appear below the device's name.
   - *If the device can't be located:* Below the device's name, "No location found" appears.
     A device's location might not be found if more than 7 days have passed since its last location was sent to Apple.

Tip: You can also play a sound on a device to help you find it.

Get directions to a device

1. In the Find My app on your Mac, click Devices.
2. In the Devices list, select the device you want to get directions to, then click the Info button on the map.
3. Click Directions.

   The Maps app opens with the directions from your location to the device's current location.

Get notified when a device is located

1. In the Find My app on your Mac, click Devices.
2. In the Devices list, select the device you want to be notified about.
3. Click the Info button on the map, then turn on Notify When Found.
   Note: Make sure you allow notifications for the Find My app.

Tip: If your device is lost or stolen, you can protect your information by marking it as lost.

Location sharing and finding devices aren't available in all countries or regions.

Accessibility

Get started with accessibility features

macOS accessibility features can help you with vision, hearing, physical motor activities, speech, and more. If you didn't turn on accessibility features when you set up your Mac, you can do so at any time in Accessibility settings.

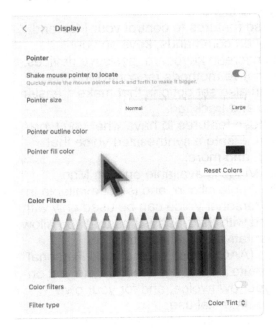

- On your Mac, choose Apple menu > System Settings, then click Accessibility in the sidebar. (You may need to scroll down.)
  In Accessibility settings, features are grouped in five broad categories on the right:
  - *Vision:* Use these features to zoom in on the screen, make text or the pointer bigger, reduce onscreen motion, and more. Or have your Mac speak what's on the screen.
  - *Hearing:* Use these features to pair Made for iPhone hearing devices with your Mac, show and customize

captions on the screen, make and receive Real-Time Text (RTT) calls, get Live Captions of audio, and more.

Note: Made for iPhone hearing devices can be paired only with select Mac computers with the M1 chip, and all Mac computers with the M2 chip. Live Captions (beta) is available only on Mac computers with Apple silicon, and is not available in all languages, countries, or regions. The accuracy of Live Captions may vary and should not be relied upon in high-risk or emergency situations.

- *Motor:* Use these features to control your Mac and apps using spoken commands, keys on your keyboard, an onscreen keyboard, assistive devices, and other alternative methods for controlling the pointer. You can also set options that make it easier to use a mouse and trackpad.
- *Speech:* Use these features to have what you type spoken out loud, create a synthesized voice that sounds like you, and more.

  Note: Personal Voice is available only on Mac computers with Apple silicon, and is not available in all languages. Personal Voice can be used only with Live Speech and with third-party apps that you allow, such as Augmentative and Alternative Communication (AAC) apps. You can use Personal Voice only to create a voice that sounds like you on device, using your own voice, and for your own personal, noncommercial use.
- *General:* Use these features to quickly turn accessibility features on or off with Accessibility Shortcuts, and to type your Siri requests.

Vision

macOS includes accessibility features that make it easier to see what's on the screen. You can also have your Mac speak what's on the screen.

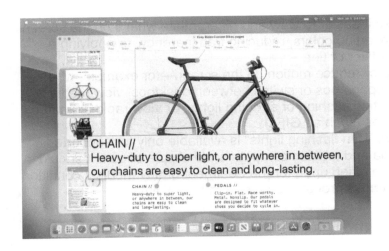

VoiceOver

Use VoiceOver, the built-in screen reader on your Mac, to speak what's on the screen, and the text in documents, webpages, and windows. With VoiceOver, you can control your Mac with the keyboard, trackpad gestures, or a refreshable braille display. To customize VoiceOver, use VoiceOver Utility.

Zoom features

- Make content on the screen larger and easier to see by zooming the entire screen or an area of it. If you're using a second display, you can set the zoom for it separately.
- Use Hover Text to see a larger version of whatever is under the pointer—for example, text you're reading or typing, or text and icons in the user interface.
- If your Mac has a Touch Bar and items in the Touch Bar are hard to see, turn on Touch Bar zoom to display a larger version of the Touch Bar on the screen.

Display features

- Use a single slider to adjust the reading size for text across multiple apps and system features.
- Make it easier to find the pointer on the screen by changing its size or color, or making it bigger when you quickly move it.

237

- Make it easier to view and differentiate what's on the screen by inverting colors, reducing transparency, or applying a color filter or tint.
- Stop or reduce motion on the screen—for example, when you open apps or switch between desktops, view media depicting flashing or strobing lights, or view rapid animated images (such as GIFs).
  Note: "Dim flashing lights" is available only for supported media and on Mac computers with Apple silicon. It should not be relied upon for the treatment of any medical condition. Content is processed on device in real time.

Spoken Content features

Customize the voice your Mac uses to speak text, and have your Mac speak announcements, items under the pointer, and whatever you type or select.

Descriptions

Listen to a description of the visual content in movies, TV shows, and other media, if available.

Hearing

macOS includes accessibility features to show and customize captions on the screen, make and receive Real-Time Text (RTT) calls, and more.

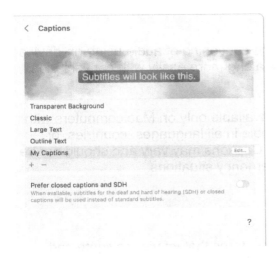

Subtitles will look like this.

Transparent Background
Classic
Large Text
Outline Text
My Captions   Edit...
+ −

Prefer closed captions and SDH
When available, subtitles for the deaf and hard of hearing (SDH) or closed
captions will be used instead of standard subtitles.

?

Hearing Devices features

Pair Made for iPhone hearing devices with your Mac and adjust their settings.

Note: Made for iPhone hearing devices can be paired only with select Mac computers with the M1 chip, and all Mac computers with the M2 chip.

Audio features

You can make the screen flash when alerts or announcements occur, and play stereo audio as mono. You can also set accessibility options for Apple earbuds and earphones paired with your Mac, and play background sounds. If you have a Mac with Apple silicon, you can choose whether Spatial Audio follows the movement of your head when you listen to Spatial Audio content.

RTT features

If your Mac supports it, set up your Mac to make and receive RTT calls.

Captions features

Control how subtitles are styled, and whether to use closed captions and SDH instead, when they're available.

Live Captions features

Your Mac can provide real-time captioning of audio using on-device intelligence so you can follow along more easily with conversations, audio, and video.

Note: Live Captions (beta) is available only on Mac computers with Apple silicon, and is not available in all languages, countries, or regions. The accuracy of Live Captions may vary and should not be relied upon in high-risk or emergency situations.

Mobility

macOS includes accessibility features that let you navigate and interact with your Mac using spoken commands, an onscreen keyboard, assistive devices, and other alternative methods for controlling the pointer. You can also set options so it's easier to use a mouse or trackpad.

Voice Control features

- With Voice Control you can speak commands to navigate the desktop and apps, interact with what's on the screen, dictate and edit text, and more.
- If the name of an item on the screen isn't apparent or you need to interact with a precise area of the screen, you can label onscreen items or show a numbered grid so it's easier to select items or navigate the screen.
- macOS provides a standard set of Voice Control commands, but you can create your own commands and use a custom vocabulary.

Keyboard features

- When you turn on Full Keyboard Access, you can navigate all UI elements on your Mac using the Tab key and other keys, instead of a mouse or trackpad.
- Sticky Keys and Slow Keys make it easier to press keys on a physical keyboard.
- When you turn on the Accessibility Keyboard, an onscreen keyboard lets you use your Mac without a physical keyboard.

It provides advanced typing (such as typing suggestions) and navigation features that you can customize for using your favorite apps.
- When you use the Accessibility Keyboard, you can turn on Dwell to perform mouse actions using eye- or head-tracking technology.

Pointer Control features

- Set options to make it easier to use the mouse and trackpad. For example, adjust the mouse or trackpad's reaction time when you double-click an item. Or drag items with or without drag lock, or with a three-finger drag.
  Alternate pointer actions let you perform mouse actions (such as a left-click or drag-and-drop action) using keyboard keys, assistive switches, or facial expressions (such as a smile or an open mouth).
- With Mouse Keys, you can move the pointer and press the mouse button using the keyboard or a numeric keypad.
- Use head pointer to move the pointer based on the movement of your face or head, as detected by the camera that's built into or connected to your Mac.

Switch Control

Switch Control lets you use one or more adaptive accessories to enter text, interact with items on the screen, and control your Mac. Switch Control scans a panel or the user interface until you select an item or perform an action using a switch.

Speech

macOS includes accessibility features to have what you type spoken out loud, create a synthesized voice that sounds like you, and more.

Live Speech

If you're unable to speak or have lost your speech over time, you can have what you type spoken out loud using synthesized speech in in-person conversations or in apps like FaceTime.

Personal Voice

If you're at risk of losing your ability to speak, you can create a synthesized voice that sounds like you.

Note: Personal Voice is available only on Mac computers with Apple silicon, and is not available in all languages. Personal Voice can be used only with Live Speech and with third-party apps that you allow, such as Augmentative and Alternative Communication (AAC) apps. You can use Personal Voice only to create a voice that sounds like you on device, using your own voice, and for your own personal, noncommercial use.

General

macOS includes accessibility features to make it easier to turn various accessibility features on or off, and to type your Siri requests.

Accessibility Shortcuts

Vision
- VoiceOver
- Zoom
- Invert Colors
- Color Filters
- Increase Contrast
- Reduce Transparency

Motor
- Sticky Keys
- Slow Keys
- Mouse Keys
- Alternate Pointer Actions
- Switch Control
- Full Keyboard Access
- Accessibility Keyboard
- Head Pointer
- Voice Control

Hearing
- Live Captions (Beta)
- Live Speech

Keyboard Shortcuts...   Settings...   Done

Siri

Type your Siri requests instead of speaking them.

Shortcut

Quickly turn various accessibility features on or off using Accessibility Shortcuts.

Accessories and hardware

Connect an external display

Depending on the capabilities of your Mac, you may be able to connect multiple displays. You may want to do this to make it easier to work in multiple programs, switch between the things you're working on, or just have more screen space.

Before you begin

Before you can connect your Mac to a display, you need to determine a few things:

- What kind of video ports your Mac has.
- How many displays your Mac can support.
- Whether or not you have the right cables.

With this information, you can connect your displays to your Mac.

Step 1: Identify the video ports on your Mac

Before you can connect displays, you need to know what type of video ports your Mac has. The ports you have determine what kind and how many external displays you can connect, and how you connect them.

Use the table below to determine what video ports your Mac has.

What it looks like	Icon	Type of port
	No icon	USB-C

⬭	⚡	Thunderbolt 3 (USB-C), Thunderbolt / USB 4, and Thunderbolt 4 (USB-C)
⬭	⚡	Thunderbolt and Thunderbolt 2
⬭	|◻|	Mini DisplayPort
⬭	HDMI	HDMI

Step 2: See how many displays your Mac supports

Next, you need to determine whether your Mac supports the number of displays you want to connect.

- *For Mac computers with the Apple M1 Chip:* You can connect a single external display to your Mac. Docks don't increase the number of displays you can connect. On a Mac mini with M1 chip, you can connect a second display to the

  HDMI port ⬭..

- *For Mac computers with Thunderbolt 3 (USB-C)* ⬭: You can connect a single display to each port. If you connect multiple Thunderbolt devices to each other, the Thunderbolt 3 display must be the last device in the chain. If your Thunderbolt 3 display has USB ports, those can be used for data and power.

- *For Mac computers with Mini DisplayPort* ⬭: You can connect up to two displays. A DisplayPort device must be the last device in a chain of connected Thunderbolt devices.

- *For Mac computers with Thunderbolt, or Thunderbolt 2* ⬭: You can connect up to two displays. If the displays themselves have Thunderbolt ports, you can connect one display to another, and then connect one of the displays to a

245

Thunderbolt port on your Mac. If your Mac has two Thunderbolt ports, you can connect each display to separate Thunderbolt ports on your Mac.

- *For Mac computers with Thunderbolt 4 (USB-C)* ▭ *and HDMI ports* ▭: You can connect up to eight external displays to your Mac, depending on your Mac model.

To get more detailed information about the type of video display your Mac supports, check the tech specs for your Mac: Choose Apple menu > System Settings, then choose Help in the menu bar. Choose [*your Mac's name*] Specifications, then scroll down to Display Support or Video Support (depending on your Mac).

Step 3: Make sure you have the right cables and adapters

- If your displays come with cables that match the ports you want to use on your Mac, you can use those cables to connect the display to your Mac.
- If your displays don't have cables, obtain cables that fit the available ports on your Mac and displays.
- If you have display cables, but their connectors don't match the ports you want to use on your Mac, you may be able to use an adapter.

Step 4: Connect your displays to your Mac

Connect your displays to your Mac using the identified video ports, cables, and adapters (if needed).

After your displays are connected, you may want to adjust their settings. Choose Apple menu > System Settings, then click Displays in the sidebar to see your displays' settings, including resolution, brightness, and color profile. You can also decide whether to extend or mirror your Mac desktop across multiple displays across your external displays.

If you have a third-party display, check the documentation that came with the display to get more information on the display's video ports and cables, and to make sure you're connecting the display according to the manufacturer's guidelines.

Use the built-in camera

Many Mac computers have a built-in FaceTime or FaceTime HD camera located near the top edge of the display. The camera automatically turns on when you open an app—such as FaceTime or Photo Booth—or use a feature—such as Markup or head pointer—that can use the camera. A green light beside the camera glows to indicate the camera is on. The camera (and the green light) turn off when you close or quit all apps or features that can use the camera.

Control access to the camera

You can decide which apps are allowed to use the camera on your Mac.

Take a photo or record a video

- *Take a photo or video of yourself.*
- *Take a photo or video of your screen.*

Improve image quality

- *Clean the camera:* Use a soft, lint-free cloth to wipe the camera.
- *Adjust lighting:* Make sure you are well lit from the front, without a lot of light behind you; for example, with windows in front of you.
- *Improve your Wi-Fi connection:* Move closer to your Wi-Fi router and make sure there are no objects impeding its signal, such as walls.
- *Change app settings:* Certain apps may allow you to adjust camera quality. Check your app settings and adjust if needed.
- *Use your iPhone as a webcam:* Connect to a supported iPhone and use its camera instead of the built-in Mac camera.

Connect a Bluetooth device

Connect your Mac with a Bluetooth® keyboard, mouse, trackpad, headset, or other audio device.

Connect a Bluetooth device

1. Make sure the device is turned on and discoverable (see the device's documentation for details).
2. On your Mac, choose Apple menu > System Settings, then click Bluetooth in the sidebar. (You may need to scroll down.)
3. Hold the pointer over the device in the list, then click Connect.
   If asked, click Accept (or enter a series of numbers, then press Enter).

You can also connect a Bluetooth device to your Mac by clicking the Bluetooth status icon in the menu bar and choosing the device. If the icon isn't shown in the menu bar, you can add it using Control Center settings.

Disconnect a Bluetooth device

1. On your Mac, choose Apple menu > System Settings, then click Bluetooth in the sidebar. (You may need to scroll down.)
2. Hold the pointer over the device in the list, then click Disconnect.

If you don't want a device to reconnect automatically, Control-click its name, then click Forget. You have to connect it again if you want to use it later.

Use AirPods with your Mac

When your AirPods are nearby and ready to use with your Mac, you can use them to listen to music, use Siri, or handle phone calls.

Pair your AirPods with your Mac

1. With your AirPods in their case, open the lid.
2. Press and hold either the setup button on the back of the case or the noise control button (on AirPods Max only) until the status light flashes white.
3. On your Mac, choose Apple menu > System Settings, then click Bluetooth in the sidebar. (You may need to scroll down.)
   Tip: To make it easier to connect your AirPods, you can add the Bluetooth status icon or Sound control to the menu bar using Control Center settings.
4. Hold the pointer over your AirPods in the list of devices on the right, then click Connect.

You can change your settings to connect your AirPods automatically or only when last connected to your Mac.

Change AirPods settings on your Mac

1. Wear your AirPods, and make sure they're connected to your Mac.
2. On your Mac, choose Apple menu > System Settings, then click the name of your AirPods in the sidebar. (You may need to scroll down.)
3. Change the controls for your AirPods. (Options vary by model.)

Optimize your Mac battery life

Your Mac is designed to be energy efficient right out of the box, using features like Compressed Memory and App Nap to stay fast and save power. However, there are several ways you can further optimize energy usage.

Note: Some of the options may not be available, depending on your Mac.

Put your Mac to sleep

When in sleep, your Mac is still turned on, but it consumes much less energy. And waking your Mac from sleep takes less time than starting it up.

- On your Mac, choose Apple menu > Sleep.

Get the most from your battery

If you have a Mac laptop, you can change the options below to reduce energy use and optimize the lifespan of your battery.

1. On your Mac, choose Apple menu > System Settings, then click Battery ▭ in the sidebar. (You may need to scroll down.)
2. Do any of the following:
   - Click the pop-up menu next to Low Power Mode on the right, then choose Always, Only on Battery, or Only on Power Adapter.
   - Click the Info button ⓘ next to Battery Health on the right, then turn on Optimized Battery Charging and "Manage battery longevity."
   - Click Options on the right, then turn on "Put hard disks to sleep when possible" and "Automatic graphics switching."

Turn your display off after inactivity

1. Choose Apple menu > System Settings, then click Lock Screen 🔒 in the sidebar. (You may need to scroll down).
2. Do any of the following:
   - Click the pop-up menu next to "Turn display off on battery when inactive" on the right, then choose an option.
   - Click the pop-up menu next to "Turn display off on power adapter when inactive" on the right, then choose an option.

Dim the display

Dim the display to the lowest comfortable level. For example, the display can be more dim when you're in a dark room than when you're in bright sunlight.

- To dim the display, press your keyboard's brightness keys or use Displays settings.
  If you're using a Mac laptop, you can also set your display to dim automatically when you're using battery power.

Turn off Wi-Fi and Bluetooth

Turn off Bluetooth® and Wi-Fi if you don't need them. They consume energy even when they aren't used.

- *Turn off Bluetooth:* On your Mac, choose Apple menu > System Settings, then click Bluetooth in the sidebar. (You may need to scroll down.) Turn Bluetooth off on the right.
- *Turn off Wi-Fi:* On your Mac, choose Apple menu > System Settings, then click Network in the sidebar. (You may need to scroll down.) Select Wi-Fi in the list on the right, then turn Wi-Fi off.

Disconnect devices and close apps

- *Accessories:* Disconnect any accessories that you aren't using, such as external hard drives.
- *Connected external drives:* If you use an external drive, such as an Apple USB SuperDrive, disconnect it from your Mac.
- *Apps:* Quit apps that you aren't using. Even an app you aren't using may be working in the background and consuming energy.

Select other energy-saving options

In Battery or Energy Saver settings, choose options that make it easier to save energy. For example, if you allow other computers to access the shared resources on your Mac—such as shared printers

251

or Music playlists—while it's in sleep you may be able to put your Mac to sleep more often.

On your Mac, choose Apple menu > System Settings, then do one of the following:

- *If you're using a Mac laptop:* Click Battery in the sidebar. (You may need to scroll down.)
- *If you're using a Mac desktop computer:* Click Energy Saver in the sidebar. (You may need to scroll down.)

Optimize storage space

macOS can help make more room on your Mac by optimizing its storage. For example, when space is needed, you can keep files, photos and videos, Apple TV movies and shows, and email attachments in iCloud, which makes them available on demand. Files don't take up space on your Mac, and you can download the original files when you need them. Recent files and optimized versions of your photos are always on your Mac.

1. On your Mac, choose Apple menu > System Settings, then click General in the sidebar. (You may need to scroll down.)
2. Click Storage on the right.

View the recommendations and decide how to optimize storage on your Mac.

Recommendations

Store in iCloud
Store all files in iCloud Drive and save space by keeping only recent files on this Mac when storage space is needed.

Store in iCloud...

Optimize Storage
Save space by automatically removing movies and TV shows that you've already watched from this Mac.

Optimize...

Empty Trash automatically
Save space by automatically erasing items that have been in the Trash for more than 30 days.

Turn On...

Recommendation	Description
Store in iCloud	Store files from your Desktop and Documents folders in iCloud Drive, store photos and videos in iCloud Photos, store messages and attachments in iCloud, and optimize storage by keeping only recently opened files on your Mac when space is needed. You can modify these settings later in the iCloud pane of Apple ID settings, Photos settings, and Messages settings.
Optimize Storage	Save space by automatically removing Apple TV movies and TV shows that you already watched, and by keeping only recent email attachments on this Mac when storage space is needed.
Empty Trash automatically	Automatically erase items that have been in the Trash for more than 30 days. You can modify this setting later in the Finder.

When space is needed on your Mac, macOS also clears caches and logs that are safe to delete, including temporary database files, interrupted downloads, staged macOS and app updates, Safari website data, and more.

Note: If your disk is partitioned, recommendations apply to only the partition that contains your home directory.

Burn CDs and DVDs

If your Mac has an external DVD drive (for example, an Apple USB SuperDrive), you can permanently store or *burn* files to CDs and DVDs to share files, move files between computers, or create backup files. Discs you burn on your Mac can also be used on Windows and other types of computers.

1. Insert a blank disc into your optical drive.
   If a dialog appears, click the pop-up menu, then choose Open Finder. Select "Make this action the default" if you want to open the Finder every time you insert a blank disc. The disc appears on your desktop.
2. Double-click the disc to open its window, then drag the files and folders you want to burn to the window.
   Aliases to the files are placed in the disc's window. The original files are not moved or deleted.
   Note: If you want to burn the same files to discs multiple times, use a burn folder.
3. Arrange and rename the files.
   When the disc is burned, the items on the disc have the same names and locations that they have in the disc window. After the disc is burned, you can't change the items.
4. Choose File > Burn [*disc*], then follow the onscreen instructions.
   The files that the aliases point to are burned to the disc. In addition, if the folders you add to the disc contain aliases, the files those aliases point to are also burned to the disc.
   Note: If you eject the disc without burning it, a burn folder with the items you copied to the disc is created and placed on your desktop. To complete the burn process later, click

   the Burn icon next to the folder in the Finder sidebar, or press and hold the Control key as you click any disc, then choose Burn Disc from the shortcut menu.

To burn a disc image (.dmg file) to a disc, Control-click the disc image file, choose "Burn Disc Image [*disc name*] to Disc" from the shortcut menu, then follow the instructions.

Tip: To erase the contents of a rewritable disc, Control-click the optical drive in the Finder sidebar, then choose Erase Rewriteable Disc from the shortcut menu.

Control accessories in your home

Accessories you add to Home are grouped in five categories along the top of the Home screen:

- Climate
- Lights
- Security
- Speakers & TVs
- Water

Below the categories, accessories are also listed individually in other sections, such as the rooms you've added.

For an introduction and ideas about using compatible smart home accessories with the Home app, click Discover in the sidebar.

Accessory categories

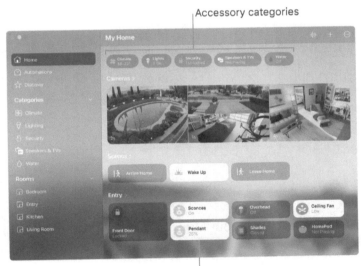

Click an accessory
to control it.

Control an accessory

- In the Home app 🏠 on your Mac, click an accessory's icon in the tile to turn it on or off. Click the accessory's name in the tile to use the available controls.
  The available controls depend on the type of accessory. For example, with some lightbulbs you can change brightness or colors. Set top boxes and streaming sticks might provide only an Activate button.

View all the accessories in a category and where they're used

- In the Home app 🏠 on your Mac, click a category at the top of the Home screen.

Control an accessory with multiple features

Accessories with multiple features are controlled by one accessory tile. For example, if you have a ceiling fan with a built-in light, you can control the speed of the fan and the brightness of the light from the same tile. Sensors are grouped by accessory categories at the top of the screen.

The available controls depend on the type of accessory.

1. In the Home app 🏠 on your Mac, click the tile of an accessory that has multiple features.
2. Click one of the features to control or view it.

Move an accessory to another room

You can add an accessory to a room or move it to another room.

1. In the Home app 🏠 on your Mac, click Home or a room in the sidebar.
2. Drag the accessory tile to a room in the sidebar.
   Tip: Control-click an accessory tile to change how the tile appears in Home.

Rename an accessory

1. In the Home app on your Mac, click Home in the sidebar.
2. Click the accessory's name in the tile, then click the Options button in the bottom-right corner.
3. Delete the accessory's name, enter a new one, then click the Close button in the top-right corner.

Use Windows on your Mac

With Boot Camp, you can install and use Windows on your Intel-based Mac.

Boot Camp Assistant helps you set up a Windows partition on your Mac computer's hard disk and then start the installation of your Windows software.

After installing Windows and the Boot Camp drivers, you can start up your Mac in either Windows or macOS.

Resources for your Mac

Get information about your Mac right on your Mac.

- *See the version of macOS installed on your computer:* On your Mac, choose Apple menu > About This Mac.
- *See your computer's specifications:* On your Mac, choose Apple menu > About This Mac. For detailed information, click More Info, then click System Report at the bottom of the window.
  For complete technical specifications, go to the Apple Support Tech Specs website — https://support.apple.com/specs. For technical specifications in other languages, click "Tech Specs in other languages" near the top of the webpage.

Made in United States
Troutdale, OR
10/26/2024